I0388149

MOTHERMARE
A MOTHERCARE NIGHTMARE

By
Ben Simon Lazarus

Published by Finesse Literary Press
http://www.finesseliterarypress.com

Copyright 2020

All rights reserved. No part of this publication may be reproduced, stored in a retrieval system or transmitted in any form or by any means, electronic, mechanical, photocopy, recording or otherwise, without prior written consent of the copyright owner. Nor can it be circulated in any form of binding or cover other than that in which it is published and without similar condition including this condition being imposed on a subsequent purchaser.

The right of Ben Simon Lazarus to be identified as the author of this work has been asserted in accordance with the Copyright Designs and Patents Act 1988.

A copy of this book is deposited with the British Library

- Disclaimer: The material in this publication is intended for an adult audience. Reader discretion is advised.
- Editors: Daniel De Kock, Aaron Kitchen, Emily Crawford-Margison

Society is an observer, it is not here to mediate or solve any mysteries. It just wants to play forever

Table of Contents

Chapter 1: Victoria Allen, I Want You to Have Everything. 5
Chapter 2: The Closure I Deserve 12
Chapter 3: The Birth of My Child 22
Chapter 4: Destroying the World — My World 36
Chapter 5: Babyhood and Beyond 42
Chapter 6: Nursery 46
Chapter 7: Primary School 49
Chapter 8: Reading Destiny's Diary 55
Chapter 9: The Jolly Goat 75
Chapter 10: What Have I Become? 87
Chapter 11: My Childhood Haunts Me 92
Chapter 12: The Secret's Out 124
Chapter 13: An Early Marriage 133
Chapter 14: My Mothercare Reality 150
Chapter 15: I Have Become My Mother 158
Chapter 16: In the News 162
Chapter 17: A Suicide Note 164

Chapter 1

Victoria Allen, I Want You to Have Everything

Notwithstanding the past, it is hard to watch her in this latter stage of her deterioration (on a human level more than anything else). My dearest elderly mother, Betty Allen, is lying in her deathbed, grasping onto the sheets as well as her final moments here on earth.

Don't get me wrong, I know we all have to go eventually. Death is merely a part of life in the end. It's an unfortunate experience we all have to come to terms with at some point, but this imminent one is really hitting home. She is my birth mother after all, you know? This is nothing like hearing or reading about someone else's tragic death on the news, however equally sad that might be. But a person you know so well going out like this... let's just say it breaks one's spirit. I guess it never feels real until you see it before your own eyes; until you experience it yourself. Although you've thought about it several times in the past, you've never physically faced it. You've never *felt* it.

My mother used to be somebody with a soul so full of fire. But now the joy that made her eyes glisten for so many years has vanished and her burning lust for life is fading away with it. She looks as if she is drowning — not in water, but in sorrow and fear. She has absolutely no control over her inevitable demise. And no one, no matter what they've done, deserves to suffer this kind of fate. Seeing her now, as she's attempting to open her puffy eyes, is incredibly difficult to watch. There is a lump in my throat and my stomach is churning.

I take a step closer to her frail, outstretched body and then my mother whispers, 'Victoria, my baby, I need to tell you something.' Her voice sounds like a dusty old bellows blower.

My attention turns to her face and I notice a single tear rolling down her left cheek. She knows exactly what is bound to happen. I wish she didn't. The pain has somehow intensified for the both of us, I now realise. These are her final moments with me. I am suffering with her. I am feeling her excruciating pain. Although our personalities are very different, I can't help but see myself as a reflection of her — a mirror image if you like. I see myself dying in a hospital bed someday. I see my life going down the same path as my mother's.

During this challenging period, I've tried to be as brave as possible but it's been tough, to tell you the truth. I'm on the verge of raising my own child as a single mother. I am nearly nine months pregnant, with only another week until my due delivery date (if my gynaecologist's calculations are correct, that is). I can imagine that this situation makes it extra hard for my dying mother, since she is so close to meeting her first grandchild. The birth of my baby would have made her very happy, especially because of my father's 'disappearance' when I was a toddler.

I'm an only child and I haven't seen much of my mother lately. Yet, I know that in her mind, her soon-to-be-born grandchild would have been her last chance to forge a close family relationship after her first failed attempt. In my mind, however, I know it is too little too late.

Staring at my mother's wrinkled face, I now see that she is unable to make eye contact with me. Her gaze is fixated on one thing only: my enormous baby bump. Not that she really has much of a choice, it's right there in her line of sight and it's humongous.

She lifts her hands from her sides and, by some miracle, manages to stretch her arms out. Grasping my belly like a vulture trying to scoop up its prey, she begins to weep while saying, 'My grandchild, you're going to have the life of my beautiful daughter. You will have everything you'll ever desire, and you will always be happy. That is a promise from Grandma.'

This is a moment I know will change everything. Although her words might sound like something from a fairy-tale to an outsider, they are daggers in my heart.

A switch suddenly triggers in my brain, as my sad childhood memories fill my mind. These memories tell a story of pain and unaccepted love, as if I were the problem as an innocent kid for all those years. I feel an emotional U-turn and my emotions turn from sadness to anger. Why should I suppress my feelings just because these are my mother's last moments with me? Deep down I know violence is never the answer, but I feel the urge to raise my hands to her.

But no, not now. Not ever. I am a better person than that; more composed and rational than that. I've held back my anger and frustration my entire life, so there is no point in exposing that to her now. I'll keep it to myself. Still, is she really that deluded to think I actually had a good life growing up? That I actually have any positive connotation with my childhood?

How could she be such a hypocrite, after all these fucking years? This monster. This... this beast. Let's be honest, she is not a mother. She is the embodiment of a demon. You know, the kind of demon we read about in the Bible. It's like I finally understand the depiction of the devil as the root of all evil. This *thing* before me is a stranger that (by some genetic connection) just happens to look a lot like me. It's a technicality, a relationship bound by biological DNA, nothing more. When I look at her malevolent face, I think of my ugly childhood and I see that she is just a ghastly old woman, exactly as I have always known her.

My utter resentment overrides any feelings of sympathy I've had earlier. Why must she be on her deathbed to finally show me even an inkling of the love that I have always deserved? Isn't that supposed to be a human right or something? I was deprived of that love. I was an angel, a blessing in her life, and she never realised it.

Thinking about her words again — 'My grandchild, you're going to have the life of my *beautiful* daughter' — I wonder if it was perhaps not my mother who said them. Maybe it was the medication and not her genuine self. Or is she truly in the midst of a realisation? Perhaps she is experiencing some sort of awareness that she cannot be buried with her possessions, and that she should have surrounded herself with family instead of her worldly belongings.

I believe that our interpersonal relationships define our legacies and the people we are. That is what we leave behind. Now she's going to lose it all. It won't be long until only her legacy remains; a legacy filled with, well, nothing — just pure emptiness and meaninglessness.

With tears stinging my eyes and anger thumping in my heart, I glare into her evil soul for what I reckon would be the last time.

I'm about to turn and leave when she says, 'Wait,' in an urgent tone.

She opens the bedside table's steel drawer to feel around for something and eventually produces a tattered, yellowing envelope. She hands it to me.

I study the text on the cold surface. My name is scrawled across the front of the envelope, above a message that says *Important Confidential Information*.

A rasping sound makes me shift my gaze back to my mother's dying figure. Her head looks heavy and her neck muscles give in as she uses her last remaining energy of the day to sink back into the crisp hospital pillow.

Staring at the fluorescent light tubes in the ceiling, she mutters her final words before nightfall: 'I love you and this is goodbye for now. Make me proud, Victoria.'

She closes her eyes and falls asleep, her snores soon echoing off the ward's walls. I know she only has days left, but I will not see her again. Without telling her I love her too, I storm out of the ward and into the waiting room, feeling lightheaded. Everything around me all of a sudden blend into a hazy blur. I am having another panic attack, something I have suffered from my whole life. Pulling up a chair, I sit down and take some deep breaths to clear my head.

After a good four minutes, I rip open the envelope and retrieve a letter with text in a legally binding format. It is titled *Last will and testament of Betty Allen*. Below this there appears only one sentence: *I hereby revoke any previous wills and codicils. I devise, bequeath and give all that I own, including my family estate, to my biological ~~grand~~daughter.*

The bottom of the page contains today's date and the monster's unsteady signature.

Chapter 2

The Closure I Deserve

Two days have passed since I last visited the hospital.

They have dragged on, actually.

I feel like a passenger, as if I'm living in someone else's skin. My time is primarily spent moping around the house, pacing around or sobbing on my favourite leather couch while looking at old family photos. I am traumatised after seeing my mother in that inferior condition. I feel drained, like an empty glass of Merlot (God, I haven't had a glass of wine in months). And, worst of all, the state of my mental health has gone from bad to horrible to rotten.

When I get like this, it's comparable to the pain of physical torture. I go through periods when I really suffer and my anxiety and depression seem to consume the person that I think I am. I know I can't allow this to spiral out of control without speaking to someone, as I've done in the past. I have to regain control. I need to see a therapist again, something I haven't done in years, let alone months.

I take out my phone, planning to find the best professional possible, but I end up calling the first number I come across. A young woman answers. Her voice is sweet. 'Hello,' is all she says. I assume this is the receptionist.

'Are you open for appointments today?' I ask urgently. Then, before she can respond to my inquiry, I shout, 'I'm coming over now! I have an emergency.' I end the call, rush to my car and drive to the address provided on the therapist's website.

Pulling into the driveway of a large residential property twelve minutes later, I notice a signboard above one of the side doors: *Professor Rupert Williams, Clinical Psychologist.*

The practice is clearly an extension of his house. The receptionist greets me as I enter. She is taller than I expected and I sense that she can tell by my urgent demeanor that I'm the woman she spoke to on the phone earlier.

'Take a seat,' she says calmly. 'The doctor will be with you shortly.' She walks into a back room, presumably to fetch him.

I get the feeling that she saw the total panic in my eyes, that I needed immediate attention, and that she was going to make me wait. Revenge, I figure. Revenge for my bluntness during the short telephone call. My body starts to feel numb. Another panic attack is on its way. Confused and dizzy, I stand up and struggle to find my balance. 'Help!' I call out. 'Someone, please help!'

The doctor hurries into the waiting room. He places a hand on my right shoulder. I can smell his cologne and it comforts me to a certain degree. 'Relax,' he says. 'It's going to be okay.' I sit down again and suck in a generous breath of air. Rupert Williams is a handsome man with dark features, I notice when I look up. Just seeing him makes me feel calmer.

Moments later, I follow him into his office, a neat room with white walls and large bay windows behind bright yellow curtains.

After asking for my name, Professor Williams gets down to business. What seems to be troubling me? Why am I distressed? Not in those words but along those lines.

I tell him about my mother; not everything but some of it. He keeps digging and digging. There is something in his eyes when he is looking at me, I realise at a point in the conversation (it feels like a *conversation* rather than a *consultation*). An emotional connection maybe? Is he fighting to keep from blushing or am I imagining it? While I'm speaking to him, our eyes lock constantly and it feels as if our souls are merging into one.

I wonder if this happens with all of his patients, because I could certainly spend a lifetime looking into those jade green eyes.

'My subconscious is forcing its way into my conscious mind,' I tell him. 'It's quite problematic, Doctor. I can hardly eat and I barely sleep at night. It feels physical, like a dozen guns are shooting at my head from different directions.' I pause to see if he'll say anything but he doesn't, so I continue. 'I suppose I just can't stand this awkward and endless agony any longer. The crushing pain feels like it'll never end...' I'm struggling to keep my thoughts together. 'My mind keeps on racing at a hundred miles per hour and the terrifying image of my mother keeps on surfacing. The reality is that I've been spending most of my time inside the house, depressed and stressed. I… I can't take this anymore, Doctor. I've always seen that light at the end of the tunnel to help me through, but for my mother, well, all I can think about is how she deserves to be set free from her suffering.'

I stop talking. The handsome Rupert Williams is still writing down notes. I find it strange that he hasn't stopped to question me about anything in over a quarter of an hour. Then I recall something else, something scary, and speak up once more. 'All of this brought me back to the days when I used to suffer growing up, and over the last couple of nights those memories triggered a recurring nightmare.'

He finally looks up from his notes. 'What? All right, tell me about this nightmare then.'

'In it, my father — Charles is his name — forgot who I was. I was about five years old and heading to my room one evening when he stopped me in the dining hall and grabbed my face. He stared straight into my eyes and sputtered out the words, "Who are you?" I told him it was me, his daughter, Victoria. He then knelt down in front of me as if I was something holy. After again staring into my eyes for a long while, he began to scream, even louder than when my mother had yelled on the phone earlier that day. The hands touching my face all of a sudden hardened. "Demon!" he kept on screaming. "Demon!" I laughed at first, but that soon stopped. "Demon, who are you?" he continued. "Reveal yourself." That was when my mother, Betty, came running into the dining hall. She took him by the wrists and pleaded for him to stop, tearing his grip away from my face. My mother then picked me up and scurried back toward the door. After putting me safely down on the floor, she went back to my father. He slapped her and called her a little bitch. This was the first time he cursed in front of me. Fortunately, my mother kept her cool and didn't lose her temper. Without saying a word, she took him by the shoulders and pulled him into the bedroom where she held him down on the bed. I watched from a crack in the door. She kept on telling him to calm down. When he finally appeared to be pulling himself together, she opened the nightstand drawer and took out a bottle of pills. She unscrewed the cap, shook a few pills into the palm of her hand and then into his mouth. Naturally, my father protested, spitting out the pills. When my mother handed him a glass of water, he violently threw it against the wall and it shattered to pieces. There were shards of glass everywhere. Aleksandra, our house cleaner, pulled me away at that point. The next day, I was told that my father had been taken away for "rest and special care" as my mother described it.'

I feel strange inner demons as I share my nightmare with Doctor Williams. These demons entered my body, I'm pretty sure of it. He sees me shivering and shaking and I know that he is terrified. Suddenly I can't stand being in the same room as him any longer and I give in to my severe anxiety. I get up, run out of his practice, and make my way home. Oddly, I have calmed down to an emotional state where I might get through the week without spending all my time panicking and impatiently awaiting the dreaded call from the hospital.

***

A few days go by and then it happens. Late in the afternoon my mobile phone vibrates with a NO CALLER ID showing on the screen.

My anxiety starts to take over again. I feel as though I am suffocating and drops of sweat are trickling down the nape of my neck. I inhale and exhale slowly as I grab my phone from the kitchen table and exit onto the veranda through the back door. I take the call outside where there is fresh air to calm my nerves. Without allowing the panic to distract me, I answer the call with a relaxed, 'Hi, this is Vicky.'

'Am I speaking to Miss Victoria Allen?' a male voice asks. I recognise it as belonging to the physician who was treating (if you could call it that in case of a dying patient) my mother.

'Is this it, Doctor?' I ask him.

And in a gentle voice, without any form of hesitation, he says, 'I have bad news for you. Unfortunately, your mother has passed away peacefully in her sleep this afternoon. I'm so sorry to be the bearer of such a grievous message.'

There is a long pause. I am temporarily speechless.

'Hello? Miss?' the good doctor says.

I simply can't bring myself to respond. All I can do at this moment is picture my mother's face in my mind's eye. I drop my phone to the floor, not even caring if the screen cracks. I then seize a framed family photo from the patio set's table and hurl it to the floor. It lands alongside my mobile phone, glass splintering. I give it a firm stomp for good measure. The anger mixed with sadness, the confusion mixed with relief, the fear mixed with hate, it all becomes too much for me. I break down like a teenage girl who had just lost her virginity without planning it. Stumbling down the stairs, I fall to my hands and knees on the patch of lawn and cry. In-between tears I hear myself say a quick prayer. 'May the Lord protect her and my family for eternity.'

I don't usually pray; I've never been particularly religious, but today it feels right. Who else can I turn to? There's no harm in it, I convince myself. Worst case scenario: no one hears my prayers and I'll be on my own to deal with my volatile emotions regardless. Best case scenario, a miracle will happen and these emotions will simply go away, vanish like mist in the sun.

My knees and arms feel weak, like jelly. I collapse onto my stomach and then roll over to my back. I remain silent and spread out my arms and legs. I lay motionless on the spongy lawn in my backyard. The grassy leaves are tickling my ears and my neck. Though it is still light outside, the moon has risen in the sky. It feels like my mind is distorting reality. I close my eyes and then say, 'One day, mother, I'll join you up there, I promise. And we will be a perfect family, just like the one we should have had. Then we'll finally have the life we deserved long ago.'

As soon as I'm finished with the pledge, something unexpected happens. I don't know what comes over me, but I suddenly start to laugh. Maybe it's a nervous reaction, like the type of response to bad news that you see in the movies or on television. But it still feels like sadness, which is okay because it's a *good* sadness. I have never experienced the relief of closure before. It feels surprisingly good, I now comprehend. A burden has been lifted, not only off my mother's shoulders but also off mine.

With my eyes still closed, I can hear the neighbours' children playing outside. When I was younger, they would sometimes linger outside my yard and snoop around. It was a game to them, an investigation. They would dress up and play detective. They'd press an eye against a small peephole in the fence that borders my garden. I could never see their faces, but whenever I heard them giggling, I knew they were there. And I can't blame them for laughing at me now. They are so young, the age when suffering can still be perceived as comical. I can picture them, watching a heavily pregnant woman flat on her back, laughing, crying and talking to herself. They must be having a field day. They must think that I recently escaped from a mental asylum.

I wipe away the tears from my face and begin to laugh once again, this time with them. Their innocence makes my soul peaceful.

As I look down at my baby bump, I feel ready to be a mother for the first time in my life. It is a wonderful feeling, almost an out-of-body experience. I love myself more than ever before. Losing someone who impacted your life so drastically was never going to be easy, I knew that from the word go. I've also realised from previous heartbreaks that these dramatic emotional events change you in many ways. And this is no different. My mother's death will mould me into a different version of myself and change my perspective until the day when it's *my* turn to die. This realisation causes me to go from resenting the moment to wanting it to last forever.

Chapter 3

The Birth of My Child

The sun is shining and there is not a cloud in the sky.

I wake up dazed and disoriented, still on the lawn in my backyard. I must have slept here the entire night because it's now early in the morning. Birds are chirping in the trees and my fingers can feel the cool dampness of dew on the grass.

While gradually rising to my feet, I gather my scrambled thoughts. It takes only a matter of seconds for me to understand that I feel completely relaxed and rested. I am optimistic about the day ahead and I can't help but smile; it's as if life has given me lemons for a jug of lemonade. Who knew closure and clarity could be the ingredients to the recipe for lemonade? I make a mental note to drink more lemonade. Life is too short and I feel alive again, for the first time in yonks. Most importantly, it seems that my attitude toward living is reshaping itself. I can finally start to think about building a future instead of always worrying about the past.

Spending valuable time to analyse one's human nature is what's really important in the path toward self-discovery and realisation. It's a blessing in disguise (a clichéd phrase, I know, but the beauty of it resonates within me). I am also aware of the following important task: now that I have momentum, I need to sustain it. I cannot allow the mourning process to trap me into a cycle of depression. I will not let my anxiety back in. Although I keep on hearing the demons knocking, I have to try and keep them at bay, deep inside my subconscious. However, like most things in life, that is much easier said than done. Thankfully, I have the best possible distraction. Today is my due date! This is *my* journey to parenthood and no one else's. It will be *my* special moment and I know I'll shine. I am not afraid to give birth to my baby — I'm going to be a strong and proud mother, I know it in my heart.

With a beaming grin on my face I walk up the stairs with the intention of going inside to take a shower and get dressed. I reach the veranda and notice the broken glass and my damaged phone on the floor. My mood suddenly begins to change. I feel negativity rushing into my head. There is still something weird going on in my mind, but I can't put a finger on it. As I start thinking back to the events that unfolded the day before, the light goes on.

I have unfinished business to take care of.

I caused a scene at Dr. Williams's therapy practice yesterday afternoon. I now feel quite embarrassed about my erratic behaviour. My attitude toward the doctor and his receptionist was rude, to put it mildly, and I know I need to make it right.

I tend to be an over-thinker in these types of situations, but today is different. Life's proverbial lemonade made sure of that. Adrenaline begins to flow through my inner being as I hurry inside. Instead of showering, I only spray two quick spurts of perfume on my neck before jumping into my car and driving to Dr. Williams's practice.

Stopping at a red traffic light four blocks from my house, I take a look at my reflection in the rear-view mirror. Are those sparkles in my eyes? Definitely. My mojo has returned. Did *his* eyes perhaps cause it? Maybe it did. I think about how our eyes met while we were having the conversation (not consultation) yesterday. The warm feeling of his hand on my shoulder, the sweet smell of his cologne. There was a special chemistry there, something that I haven't felt since my ex, Peter, and I broke up.

Am I going crazy?

Who knows?

The little angel's voice inside my head starts speaking. *Let's be honest here, Victoria, he hardly even said anything to you yesterday afternoon.*

Then the little devil's voice takes over. *But his presence, his beautiful green eyes, lavish hair and well-defined jaw… what else can a girl do but get lost in his beauty?*

And I could sense it, couldn't I? When he looked at me, the curve of his mouth, almost like he wanted to say something a little more personal to me… but then he would stop himself, quickly remembering that he was the therapist and I was the patient. It was still unclear yesterday when I was a mess, but now it all makes perfect sense. Perhaps that is why I flew out of the practice like a tracer bullet yesterday — I was afraid of his charisma. Not anymore, though. I need to see him again and it's not only to apologise for my bad behaviour.

Come to think of it, this isn't only about the undeniable raw physical attraction between the two of us. He seemed to know all about me and the way my emotions were manifesting. Furthermore, he wasn't fazed at all by the disturbing nature of my deepest, darkest secrets.

I now find myself asking the key question of the moment: What if he is the guy I'm meant to be with? The soulmate to spend the rest of my life with? God knows I could do with some love and happiness. After everything that I've been through with my mother, I deserve some luck. I deserve life to give me a bit of a break, you know?

My little moment of daydreaming is rudely interrupted by the car behind me. I mean, how many times does anyone need to blow the horn? I drive on and make a hasty stop at the next gas station I see. I don't need petrol, but I want to pick something up for Dr. Williams. Thankfully, they sell flowers and I choose the nicest bouquet they have, which is merely the best of a pretty sorry selection. I comfort myself by thinking, at the very least, he will appreciate the gesture more than anything else.

***

When I reach his practice, I hop out of my car in excitement but pause at the door, in the shadows of the massive trees lining the front yard. I peek through one of the windows. The lights are all switched off but it's rather early, perhaps he is still sleeping. I knock anyway, since I need to know if my instincts are right.

A minute goes by and nobody answers the door. However, I'm not going to just give up this easily. Like they say: desperate times call for desperate measures. I put my right hand on the brass doorknob and turn it while pushing forward. No luck. The door doesn't open. I figure my only remaining option is to keep my head down and walk back to my car.

Looking at my baby bump and the flowers in my left hand, a vision all of a sudden pops into my head. It's an image of Dr. Rupert Williams cradling our baby in our living room. While he is gently rocking our baby back and forth, I, his wife, Mrs. Victoria Williams, walks up to him and places a soft hand on his firm shoulder. It will be real love. And, just like the demons inside me, love for yours truly is all-encompassing. It completely engulfs me and takes over who I am. Sometimes I wish it wouldn't, because it usually results in a moment of madness…

And that is exactly what is about to happen.

There is a special connection between us. I just know it. That is why I now position myself to get a better view of any alternative entry points into his house.

I instantly see one.

Just my luck, of course. The entry point in question is an open window on the second floor of the house. But love holds no bounds, I can do this. Although I am a realist and know I'm not Spiderman, I also know that I am capable of almost anything, pregnant or not. I'll go into full stealth mode, like an oversized ninja. Wait, no, that's not going to work... I don't want any spectators to assume that I'm an intruder. If I forget about the stealth and merely act casual, I will simply appear to be an innocent pregnant lady who has been locked out of her home.

Have you gone stark raving mad, Victoria? the little angel's voice inside my head says.

She's right, of course. This plan just isn't going to be worth all the trouble. Besides, I'm wearing a knee-length shirt. What if some poolboy or gardener looks up while I'm busy climbing to the top? No, before potentially falling from the second floor (or being humiliated by some poolboy), I should try the back door.

If, by some chance, it has been left open, I will take it as a sign from God that Rupert and I are meant to be together. If it is locked, then I'll throw away the stupid flowers and forget any of this ever happened. I am leaving it up to fate. My destiny is now in the hands of the universe, or the stars, or whatever.

I sneak around the side of the building and locate the pedestrian gate that separates Dr. Williams's front garden from the pathway leading to the back. So far, so good — the gate is unlocked. I open it and walk through, cautiously glancing around for any signs of dogs or other pets that could expose my presence. As I approach the backyard, I notice that there is a glass conservatory extension built onto the back of the house.

This is when our eyes meet for the second time. He looks hot in jeans and a t-shirt but, unlike yesterday, Rupert seems off. I can't tell exactly what it is, but he appears tired and angry.

My suspicion about the angry part is confirmed when he slowly picks up an aluminium baseball bat. I figure he must be fuming and the unfriendly greeting that follows once again confirms this feeling.

'Don't take one step further,' he says loudly, 'or I'm calling the police.'

Freezing in my tracks, I raise my hands above my head while saying, 'No, no, no, this is just a little misunderstanding,'

'What the hell are you doing?' he continues, tapping the bat on the conservatory's tiled floor. 'First, you've woken me up, and now you're trespassing on my property! What is wrong with you, woman?'

He seems really livid. But would he actually hit one of his patients with a baseball bat? Surely not, especially not one of his *pregnant* patients. I call his bluff and start to close the distance between us until I reach the open door, still clutching the flowers. I'm now only ten feet away from the handsome Dr. Williams. He is just standing there, twitching his mouth while gripping the bat so tight that his knuckles are turning white.

I can't handle it to see him like this. He's too gorgeous to be this mad. But wait, is there something else in the expression on his face? Ah, yes, I see it… even though he's hiding it very well, he appears to be pleasantly surprised by my early morning visit. I know now more than ever that I will bring him so much happiness in future that it'll make up for this day. We'll look back on this day and laugh about it together with our kids.

'Rupert, my love, put it down,' I say in my kindest voice.

'M-my l-love?' he stammers back. 'What do you mean, *my love*?'

The time is right, I decide. 'Rupert, there is something I have been meaning to tell you. Something I need to get off my chest. When I saw you for the first time yesterday, I felt a connection between us. I don't know if you felt it, too.'

His anger turns into confusion as he looks at me and replies, 'A connection? What sort of a connection?' He puts the baseball down on a nearby table.

Without saying anything in return, I step closer and then boldly walk into the house, my shoes clicking on the tiles like a lazy rattlesnake on a warm summer day.

He doesn't move away. I flutter my eyelids and give him a look of seduction. He still doesn't step back. I can tell he's feeling comfortable. He wants this. We are now only inches away from each other. He smells nice. While giving me a curious stare, he delicately places a hand on my shoulder. I run my fingers down his naked arm. I glance up at his lips.

We kiss.

I knew it!

It's a wonderful feeling of joy and love. He places his hands on my hips and we kiss again. Deeper and more purposeful this time.

'What the fuck are you doing with my husband, you psychopathic bitch?'

Our intimate moment gets smashed to pieces. It's the receptionist from yesterday.

Dr. Williams immediately pushes me away and we stand there in silence.

'Rupert, what the hell is this whore doing in our house?'

Dr. Williams responds calmly by saying, 'Honey, she broke in and forced herself on me. It all happened so fast.'

He isn't particularly convincing, so I have to step in. 'It's not what it looks like,' I begin. 'Funny story, actually. I came over to apologise.' I hold out the flowers. 'These are for you.'

She glares at me. 'This is your way of saying sorry, you disgusting pig?'

It is at this moment that I go into labor.

'I think my baby is about to be born!' I say in a blind panic.

Dr. Williams looks at me and then at his wife before saying, 'We need to get her to a hospital right away.'

I have made preparations in the best possible way, yet I'm still frightened. Over the past nine months my priority has always been to ensure that my baby will be happy and healthy. Like all mothers-to-be, this is the most important thing in my life right now. I've drawn up an extensive birth plan. I knew I would need high-quality care, so I've made arrangements with a private hospital not far from my house. I don't trust the National Health Service. Only the best of the best will be good enough for my darling baby.

On my way to the hospital (in the backseat of Dr. Williams's car) I contact my midwife, Lucille, and tell her that I'm on my way.

Upon arrival at the hospital's maternity ward, Dr. Williams and his wife, as well as the hospital staff do a great job in calming me down. This will turn out to be a short-lived comfort though. I know that the moment I'm alone again, the demons will come rushing back and my depression and anxiety will consume me once more. Nonetheless, I find myself smiling. I have a realisation, a clarity to my thoughts that I haven't had before. My cute little baby will become my companion and my permanent source of happiness. I will never be alone again.

The birth itself is, well… eventful for me but uneventful for everyone else around me. Unlike me, they do this for a living.

Anyway, the next thing I know, I am cradling a beautiful baby girl in my arms. The pure happiness I'm experiencing is too much for me to process. I feel complete. It's like when I win in a computer game, except I can't just dispose of these feelings like I do with my games when I get bored. This mother-child relationship will be ongoing. Forever.

I look up and see that it's only me and my midwife in the private hospital room.

'Hey, Lucille,' I say to her, stroking the forehead of my bundle of joy. 'Do you mind if we have a moment alone? Just me and the baby?'

'Not at all. Take as much time as you need.' She exits the room, leaving the door ajar.

I gaze into my baby's eyes. They look like mine. She is my cub, and it is my responsibility to protect her. I shed a tear while thinking about my mother's death. I don't want history to repeat itself. I don't want my daughter — or any future children for that matter — to look at me the way I looked at my mother. I want them to remember me for giving them a good upbringing, for inspiring them, and for encouraging them to blossom into something we could all be proud of.

I think of my baby's innocence. She's a blank canvas, a sponge ready to soak in the knowledge of the world. I will not allow money to jeopardise that.

The money from the inheritance of my mother's estate is the main catalyst behind my pain and frustration. I have made a conscious decision not to follow in Betty Allen's footsteps. My children will never have money — I won't let them. Money and suffering go hand-in-hand, that much I've learned over the years. I know first-hand that money also creates artificial happiness, and I want to keep that as far away as possible from my children. They will only know genuine happiness and heartfelt love. My baby will spend her life experiencing only true, authentic love and joy.

I promise her she will never suffer the pain that I have endured as a child.

Her name will be Destiny.

Chapter 4

Destroying the World — My World

It has been a number of days since Destiny's birth. Dr. Rupert Williams never contacted me again, but I don't have the time to mourn the loss of what could have been. All I can think about is the promise I've made to my daughter. At the moment I'm trying my utmost best to think of a way to press my life's restart button. I know I need a fresh start — and I need it *now*. You know what they say: 'Every story comes to an end, and thus, inevitably, a new beginning is born.' Granted, I don't know who exactly said that, but people always say these kinds of things.

Upon returning home from the hospital, it was very obvious that nothing in my life would ever be the same again. The act of giving birth was, in some ways, the way I imagine a religious person experiencing a spiritual awakening. I finally have the clarity I've always wanted. But talk is cheap. At the end of the day, our actions define us.

I am now holding Destiny in my arms in the living room of my monster mother's mansion and I begin to breastfeed her. On the wall is an old family portrait. It is of myself, my mum, and my dad. I'm noticing for the first time that my smile is fake in the picture.

So at this moment, I give it some thought as I shift my gaze from the portrait to my darling Destiny. I come to the conclusion that I have to destroy everything I previously had in an attempt to rebuild my life and carve a future for my baby girl. My next move will be to transition my materialist mindset into one of complete minimalism. My logic is this: I don't exactly remember when, but I was watching this American TV show once and the characters were talking about what I thought was a strange ritual at the time. They said that when couples break up they should destroy all evidence that they were ever together in a bonfire-type ceremony.

Thinking about the purpose of such an act, it seems as if I must fuel the flames with anything that reminds me of a specific person, which, in this case, is my mother. I know the bonfire ritual is applicable to my current circumstances. The chief objective will be to successfully erase all traces of my time with her, in order to create space for time with Destiny.

In a break-up situation, according to the TV show, the main ingredients to be included in this special ceremony's recipe are tears, photos and belongings of the ex-lover, and, of course, lighter fluid. All of this goes onto a bonfire and after that it's easy. Light a match, then sit back and watch the memories burn to ashes. Ashes that will be blown away by the wind or perish in the rain. Apparently, after completing this act, you feel like an entirely new person. There's no harm in trying it, right?

Before I do anything, I think about what I'm going to do with the house and all the inheritance money my mother has signed over to me. I have millions to my name, all of it in crisp banknotes stored in the attic of my mansion. When I was young, my parents came up with an idea of a walk-in safe for their cash. They never trusted banks or other financial institutions. Now I'm sitting with that legacy and I have to find a way to get rid of it without attracting too much attention; something that is once again easier said than done.

The last thing I want is for Destiny to even enter this toxic environment, and I do my best to ignore the fact that she already has. My first consideration is to get rid of the keys to this monstrosity and start looking for a new house; a modest one, more in line with my new perspective on life. I also know this needs to be done swiftly and efficiently.

I reach the implementation phase in my mind. Step one is to find a safe place for Destiny while I work my magic. After giving her a big, sloppy kiss on the forehead I drop her off at a reliable babysitter Lucille has recommended. The next step is to pack. I rummage through the house and bundle every sentimental item that reminds me of Betty Allen and my previous life into cardboard boxes. Truth be told, I don't find a lot of stuff. My mother wasn't a hoarder and she wasn't very sentimental either (not surprising, given her cold heart). On top of that, we didn't tend to do much together as a family that would constitute it being worth capturing in a photograph, so there also aren't a ton of pictures around. I throw everything into the back of my Fiat 500, a car I bought myself last year using the family credit card.

Dusk is approaching when I eventually pull out of the driveway and begin my journey to materialistic destruction. I attach my phone to the car's mounting unit and map my way to the nearest landfill.

When I reach the spot, I park behind a tower of rubbish hidden from view of the public's eyes. I climb out and leave everything in the Fiat, including my house keys. All I take with me are the clothes on my back and my special bag, containing Destiny's things and a few of my personal items like toiletries, underwear and my purse with one credit card. The next step is to cover my car in lighter fluid and cooking oil. I leave a trail so I can light it from a safe distance.

After a final, condescending glance at my makeshift bonfire, I toss a match and light up my history with the evil Betty Allen.

Hallelujah, motherfucker!

The flames burn fast and follow the trail of fluid and oil like a cheetah chasing a deer. There is not even a hint of a breeze in the air and it is now almost completely dark. While hugging my shoulders thirty yards from the fire, I hold my breath, waiting for the big boom that will be created once the gas tank ignites and explodes.

Seconds later it happens. Not a boom, but a loud BANG!

The force of the blast knocks me to the ground, but it makes setting ablaze every piece of my mother's history utterly satisfying. It's a dream come true.

Brushing off my clothes and rising from the ground, I watch the materialistic pile burn furiously for five minutes, slightly surprised at my bravado. Then I call a cab and begin to walk away from the flames.

I will never look back.

A new chapter in my life has begun.

Chapter 5

Babyhood and Beyond

I, Brenda Allen, have successfully carried Destiny Allen through babyhood on Tower Hamlets, a tranquil council estate in Lansbury. What a story that would be! I have heard that the community over here is a closely-knit one and that these people don't define themselves by their earthly possessions. So I changed my first name to Brenda and moved house. Victoria wouldn't roll off the tongue as well in this mediocre estate, believe me, I've done my research.

The first two years of motherhood turned out to be one heck of a ride. I have immersed Destiny in a totally different upbringing than the one I'd had. A lot of my success as of right now is due to my initial 'statement of purpose.' I am doing everything in my power to be absolutely nothing like my mother. This is because whenever Destiny and I are faced with a difficult situation or a crossroad, I deal with it by asking myself, 'What would my mother have done?' Then I do the exact opposite. Clever, don't you think? It's quite liberating and it has been working out rather well. Which is good, because these vital years of growth, some argue, are amongst the most important parts of our lives.

A constant reminder to myself is the following: If I could get through my own childhood, which was tough, I can certainly help Destiny get through hers. And while I'm doing this, I will make sure my daughter is primed to handle the classic deprived societal trap. It's a vicious cycle, really; once you enter, it is nearly impossible to escape. Community institutions and societal constructs are so inherently entrenched in popularity that, statistically speaking, she will never escape the vicious cycle. Fortunately, I have made peace with that. But what I won't budge on is the materialistic issue. Destiny will enjoy the smaller things in life and, most important of all, she'll never have money to mess up her life.

Okay, so I can pretend that everything is going great because I'm acting differently from my mother. But the reality is that it hasn't all been a breeze. Babies, they seem so cute on the outside. I mean, come on, they're adorable, even irresistible at times. Just looking at their puffy cheeks, squishy faces and large round eyes is like being hypnotised. But I have learned not to allow their endearing exterior features to deceive me. On the inside, they are evil little creatures.

What I'm talking about here is the other side of the coin: the wet and dirty nappies, the endless crying, and the constant need for attention. All of that can take its toll on you, physically, mentally and emotionally. Raising a child is an around the clock job that no one quite understands unless they've been through it. I have to cope with sleep deprivation, constantly running after her, and not having any time to myself. It's enough to drive a person completely insane. It's also probably the catalyst that caused my mother to go crazy... Wait, who am I kidding? She was off the rails long before I was born. Ask my dad, if can find him on this godforsaken planet.

But the hard work I invest into Destiny's babyhood is all worth it when I see her smile. It's better than any drug and it helps me forget about the times when I want to pull my hair out. To help myself out a bit, I've bought Destiny some dolls to play with. Nothing expensive, just the entry level dolls you can find at any toy store. They make her particularly happy and I recently started purchasing her many more. They create a good distraction when I'm not available, busy doing house chores or cooking food. She loves her dolls so much and when she plays with them she misbehaves less, maybe because she doesn't feel as lonely. I get to watch her form a special emotional attachment to these dolls as the days go by...

***

Tomorrow Destiny will enter the nursery as a three-year-old toddler.

The doll addiction is prominent as ever. Not that it's a problem, yet. She's given them names and she refers to them as her best friends. Personally, I think it's healthy for a child to use their imagination and play house like this, especially when they feel alone. She still has no siblings. When I'm unable to give her attention, I reckon that it's better for her to play with her dolls than to sit and watch the dumb invention called television, like all the other kids do.

Chapter 6

Nursery

My social media profiles are filled with self-proclaimed 'yummy mummies.' It's almost impossible to escape the societal pressure, no matter where you go. People paint pictures that their lives are so perfect. Stunning women post digital photos where they are posing with their beautiful children, while teenagers brag about their 'awesome' parents.

It's starting to affect me more than it should. I know this because I'm addicted to watching their lives unfold through daily vlogs. It makes me feel as though I'm not good enough. And that somewhere, somehow, I'm going in the wrong direction. I wouldn't say I'm jealous, but I still keep on asking myself, 'Why can't it be me who is so damn perfect?'

Whenever I visit Destiny's nursery, I can't help but notice how confident and well put-together the other mothers are. They appear to be happy, calm and (most surprising of all) well-rested. I have also observed something else — all these mothers look very different to my friends' mums when I grew up, attending an expensive private school. I don't know if it is really the case, but they give off the impression that their lives are much easier than mine. In my mind and in my heart I know that the issue isn't that they are better mothers than I am. Because I cannot for the life of me think that anyone could possibly care better for a child than I do for Destiny. I'm beginning to suspect that the issue has something to do with the fact that most of these 'other mothers' have good-looking, strong, supportive husbands by their sides, whilst I have no such luxury.

The truth of the matter is that these mums are so put-together because they don't have nightmares plaguing them each night. They focus on their own appearances and on presenting their families in the best light. Nonetheless, it puts a pep in my step to realise that I am doing what the other mothers do, but without the help of a partner. I will hold my head high knowing that I have what they don't — self-respect, courage, and the ability to do this alone.

I give myself a lot of credit for what I've done without a man in my life over the past few years. And believe me, every mother at that school will hear how amazing I've been with Destiny's upbringing. I'll be one of those infamous mothers who will never be forgotten at their child's school. Actually, come to think of it, I should be nominated for some kind of Mothercare award. How couldn't I be proud of what I have achieved so far? I'm honoured to call myself Supermum. In addition to the award nomination, I also deserve one of those *World's Best Mum* coffee mugs, as a daily reminder of my top-quality parenting skills.

Chapter 7

Primary School

It's Destiny's first day in primary school. How exciting!

Her babyhood and toddler days have really gone by like a flash. I look at her now and I'm amazed at how much she has grown. Her flowered frock is neatly pressed and her polished shoes shine like diamonds. She is patting her braided hair to make sure every strand is in place. Destiny will enter her reception class with dignity, her dolls as her best friends.

A month ago I bought myself an old banger for the school runs. The car is a total piece of crap, but it's still kind of roadworthy. As long as it gets us from one place to the other, I can't complain. Sure, from time to time it does give me tremendous stress, particularly when the engine sounds like it's about to explode, but that's all part of living a minimalist life. And yes, I've indulged in a few luxuries for the sake of comfort, because I don't want to be perceived as piss poor by others who might interpret minimalism as a reflection of monetary status. I want my daughter to fit in and have friends after all. But any impending expense first undergoes the test of practicality and responsibility. With my new lifestyle everything is about appreciating what I already have instead of wanting more.

When we arrive at the school, we are the first ones outside the gates. I see the anxiety in Destiny's eyes. I give her a cuddle and tell her, 'It'll be alright, pumpkin. You're so strong, you can do anything.'

I chat to the other parents as they congregate outside the classrooms. The conversations go swimmingly. One of the mothers introduces herself as 'The Strawberry.' I hope it is only a reference to her red hair, but I can't make any assumptions with these people. She seems lively, a real social butterfly with a bubbly personality. She informs me that she works as a waitress at the local pub, the Jolly Goat. She has a lot more personality than she does teeth.

It's all going wonderful, but at some point I notice that the mothers around me are starting to cover their mouths with their hands or purses. They pull their children close to them. They appear to be afraid of something or someone.

Strawberry lady taps my shoulder and points to an area behind me.

I turn around and see a man covered in tattoos. 'Who is that?' I ask.

'That's Billy. He's the creep that roams around outside the school gates.'

I've never heard anything about this Billy before. He doesn't have a child with him. He is just standing there by himself, glaring at the mothers. I turn back to Strawberry. 'Watch Destiny for me,' I tell her. 'And watch this.'

I walk toward him.

'Be careful!' Strawberry calls out.

When I reach Billy, I say, 'Hi, my name is Bren…' But before I can finish he takes my hand and kisses my wrist. There it is again — that same emotion I experienced when I first met Dr. Rupert Williams. I have to fight to keep my knees from buckling.

'It's a pleasure to meet you,' he says with a smile. 'I'm Billy. You must be Beautiful.'

He is incredibly charming and I feel flattered. It's been so long since any guy has paid attention to me. I have a deep intuition inside me that this might be the start of something special. Now that the Dr. Williams ship has sailed, it's time to get back into the game. In fact, I feel it so strongly, it's like I have no choice in the matter.

'What are you doing here at the school, Billy?' I ask him.

'Oh, I'm the new football coach,' he replies with flushed cheeks. 'Sorry if it seemed like I was acting weird. I was only employed this week, so I've been inspecting the school grounds over the last couple of days. They haven't given me the keys to the sports equipment building yet. I'm actually waiting on the headmaster...' Billy grins, stealing a glance at the other mums behind me. When he returns his gaze to me, I feel his eyes burning into mine. 'I have to admit,' he says, chuckling, 'it is a little funny to see them freaking out like that.'

Turning my head to take a look over my shoulder, I see that Strawberry is staring at us and I suddenly feel a burst of confidence. I may have let the last one get away, but that's not going to happen this time. I know we're on the same level, so I decide to go for it.

'I can think of something that will *really* freak them out,' I say to Billy. My eyes are now focussed on his lips. I pull him toward me and give him the biggest French kiss I have in me. The warmth of my lips is received by his, as if he were expecting it. I wait, anticipating some kind of reaction from behind me, but the shriek I hear is not in the right tone.

'Come back here!' someone screams.

I spin around on my heels, only to see Destiny chasing a black kitten, heading straight for the street. Billy runs after her before I can make a move. He reaches her in time and picks her up, then he brings her back to me. I grab Destiny's hand and hold it tight. 'What is wrong with you, Destiny Allen?' I ask her. She looks down with trembling lips.

'Maybe I can help,' Billy tells me. He crouches and says, 'Hi, Destiny. My name is Mr. Stevenson. I'm the new football coach. I saw how fast you ran and I think you have what it takes to make the team. How does that sound?' He bumps her shoulder with a tattooed elbow.

Destiny glances up and smiles at him.

I look at Billy. *And* he's good with kids? I think. This surely is the man of my dreams. He's invited Destiny into his life and, in doing so, me as well. Besides, since moving to Lansbury, I've become infatuated with guys covered in tattoos. I need a man with ink sleeves and he's got it. And, most importantly, Destiny seems to like him.

***

Several months pass and Destiny is now on the football team.

She is excited about her after-school practice, like always. She ties her shoe laces while saying, 'Mummy, one day I want to be like those professional footballers I've seen on the television.'

I laugh and then remind her about the importance of listening to her coach in order to achieve greatness. Destiny never questions the special treatment she's receiving from her football coach. She is absolutely oblivious, but it makes her feel special. Under normal circumstances, she wouldn't be picked in the football team at all; she's not very athletic. But she keeps excelling because of Billy's urging inspiration. She's so young and naive that she doesn't question her limited abilities.

In the evenings, Destiny regularly sees her coach walk out of her mother's bedroom wearing nothing but a towel. In these situations, she always runs over to him in excitement and hugs him. Destiny feels comfortable having her football coach in our house.

'He must really think I'm a great player,' she's told me over breakfast on many occasions. 'That's why he keeps on coming back here to see me. I'm so lucky!'

Chapter 8

Reading Destiny's Diary

Destiny's eleventh birthday is a magnificent occasion, just like all of her previous birthdays. Billy and I made sure of it. We told the entire estate, so that we could all celebrate as one big family. We organise a massive street party and a lot of people join us.

There are balloons, clowns, a live band and plenty of snacks as well as mango punch. Destiny doesn't seem particularly happy, though. I think it's because of the lack of school friends that turned up. There are more adults than kids at the party and she must be feeling unpopular with her peers. That kind of feeling will upset any child. But it's just a part of growing up.

She is due to go to high school soon, so I don't worry too much about her lack of friends. In fact, I think Billy and I are doing a stellar job of helping Destiny feel loved and appreciated. Not only do we give her our time and attention, but this year we also give her a special new doll as a present. This one can cry actual tears and has a speaker inside to make it laugh or sneeze. My daughter absolutely adores it. The 'high-tech' doll becomes her new best friend. However, this present is just an appetizer prior to the main course. Billy and I went all out this year... within reason, of course.

Now, because I'm still following my anti-materialist mentality, I believed that Destiny deserved something a bit more sentimental. So, we bought her a diary for her birthday. This gift will provide a platform for her to communicate her feelings to herself without the fear of being judged by others, including me. It will be like therapy for her. Billy sees her as an outcast who is merely trying to find herself and her place in this scary and confusing world. Recently, we have been under the impression that she is going through one of those dreaded phases we'd been fearing for years: becoming a teenage brat. We hope it will pass quickly.

The warm summer weeks eventually lead up to her first day at secondary school. Destiny wants to take one of her dolls with her as a friend, but she's too old now I explain to her. I can't let her odd behaviour spoil such a landmark occasion for the family. Billy and I confiscate the doll so that she won't be bullied at school. Kids can be so cruel sometimes.

***

Four months later, I'm standing in the kitchen one afternoon when Billy says, 'Brenda, you might want to sit down for this.'

The words that are coming out of his mouth are troubling for a number of reasons. The most pressing concern is the uncharacteristically formal approach he is taking. Usually he doesn't take *anything* serious and he never calls me Brenda (I'm either sweetheart, honey or darling). There is also a worrying look in his eyes. An expression I've never seen before.

He pulls out a chair and waits for me to sit. Then he takes a seat on another chair across the kitchen table from me. I look at him with a frown. When he doesn't say anything, I break the silence. 'Just spit it out already, Bill. What's the matter?'

He knows that I'm not messing around. That I need the truth, that I deserve the truth, and that I deserve to hear it right now.

After a long minute he says, 'Destiny, well…' He pauses briefly. 'I found out she's been skipping school. Principal Turner informed me. One of the other students reported it to him.'

I can't believe my ears. 'What? Are you sure? How long has this been going on for?'

'Her last few weeks as a primary school student, she missed them,' he tells me in a voice barely above a whisper. 'She even skipped leavers day.'

It's difficult to accept as the truth. Leavers day is the last day before the primary school students move to secondary education. It is a fun-filled day for the kids. Instead of going to class they watch movies, eat junk food and sign each other's school uniforms. It's a big *hoo-ha*, a kind of a goodbye-and-good-luck day. I can't believe she would miss out on such a special occasion. The two single-word questions that come up in my mind are *Why?* and *Where?* *Why* would she miss such a special day? *Where* was she? Was she with someone? And, if so, who?

We confront her but she refuses to give us answers. After a few days we let it go.

***

Throughout the rest of the year Destiny doesn't go out much. She spends most of her time in her bedroom with the door locked. It's such a shame, because it's hard to imagine her being cooped up all alone in her room, which isn't very spacious. We try to encourage her to play with the other teenagers living on the estate, but she declines our suggestion. She even makes a cardboard DO NOT DISTURB sign that she hangs on the doorknob outside her room. Something doesn't add up because I always hear talking in there. For someone without friends, that's just strange. I can't understand it and I don't think she would simply be talking to herself.

Billy suspects she might have a secret boyfriend she isn't telling us about. We consider this. Maybe she calls him or sneaks him into her room through the window without us knowing. It's rather worrying for me and Billy, the prospect of Destiny hiding something from us.

It's also difficult to conceive what my daughter must be going through. I wish I could understand what is going on. Each day I see more and more of my own childhood in her, in the way that she moves through the house and out the door. We keep on asking ourselves why she looks so miserable whenever she returns home from school. It feels to us as if both her childhood innocence and her lust for life are fading away at a rapid pace.

Whatever the hell is going on needs to be addressed before it spirals out of control. Lansbury is known for its high crime rate and we just want to make sure Destiny is safe.

She was capable of skipping primary school, even under Billy's surveillance. She could be capable of anything. She is my daughter after all. But that doesn't mean I can simply trust her unconditionally. The little devil's voice inside me tells me to let her struggle a bit. For once, the little angel agrees. Yes, it will make her stronger.

But the last thing I need, we need, is for this teenage girl to hurt herself in some way. I'm between a rock and a hard place here. If I do nothing, she might get damaged, and if I do something, I might drive her away. The latter seems to be the better option.

Drastic measures are required.

We decide we need to know where she is at all times; constant tracking. It's a shame that it's unethical to implant a GPS tracking device into a child without their consent. In the 'real world,' though, I think I might have a plan. As a parent I need to understand what she is doing while she is meant to be in the classroom, learning. It is my obligation as a mother to find out everything about my daughter. My mother wouldn't have cared a rat's ass, and that enough is an incentive for me to care the most. To me, this is motherhood — looking out for your daughter.

I nervously go to her bedroom one morning when she's out of the house. The DO NOT DISTURB sign is on her door, so I'm a little hesitant to just barge in. My hesitation lasts all of thirty seconds. When I enter, I see a big mess. Clothes and pencils and sheets of paper are scattered across the floor. Destiny's dolls are sitting in miniature chairs, bedside a tiny table in her dollhouse. It almost feels like I've interrupted an imaginary tea party. I didn't know that she still played with her dolls. I get lost in the thought for a short while, but then I'm back on track. My mission is to find something specific to read. The particular piece of literature that I am interested in is a book called Destiny's Diary. I find it inside the drawer of her bedside table. Picking it up, I flip open to the first page and then start reading.

It says the following

This is my personal diary and, whoever you are, I'd appreciate it if you could show some respect and close it immediately.

If you are still reading, now again is your chance to stop...

So, you're still reading?

You should know that I have placed a curse on the evil sleuth who finds pleasure in sticking his or her nose into someone else's personal business. By even opening this diary you have shown a clear intent to read through my secrets, so writing down a note asking you not to continue reading is comparable to politely asking a bully to refrain from doing their bullying, straight after they've punched you in the face. Clearly these warnings can't safeguard my secrets from you. But mark my words, be careful. If you choose to read on, you have taken a step closer to entering my mind, which I find to be rather delusional. What you find it to be is up to you.

I lower the diary. It simply isn't normal behaviour for a kid in high school to be writing like this. My daughter obviously has a lot to hide. And yet, her warnings are nothing more than futile. I hope she knows that. If she doesn't, it's most probably because she's been skipping school.

I look back at the diary. There is an element of intrigue in these pages. I read on

My life is a rollercoaster of emotions. It is confusion thrown into disarray, amounting to something driven only by constant energy and effort. I want to blossom but I can't. My mind is different and perhaps so is my honesty. I can't really tell.

I am like a flower, a beautiful flower, struggling against the wild rains of a world that fails to understand or appreciate me.

The more I read, the more disturbing it becomes. It makes me question not only Destiny's character and self-worth, but also my own. Am I a failure as a mother? A child shouldn't be communicating in this manner. It's so... well, pessimistic. I read on nevertheless

I don't think people really understand me. Because my peers cannot not comprehend my strong, silent presence, they try to avoid

me. I use my dolls as props and my bedroom as a prison to isolate me from their infantile behaviour.

I realised this a while ago when I locked myself in my bedroom on a day when some so-called friends were hanging out at our house during a party Billy organised. I finally grew up then. I became a woman and a nurturer. I was also really close to my dolls on that day. I kept them secure and clean and they kept me company. They would never deceive me. I brushed their hair carefully, as if they had real hair, and I told them how much I loved them.

Sometimes, I have to convince myself that my dolls are just that — dolls. But they are not only dolls to be displayed in my room. Whenever I take them out of my closet, I am touched by the way they stare at me with those long-lashed, fragile eyes. They are dolls, all right. They are my dolls. I made a fort out of their big boxes and hid myself inside it on the day that I became a woman. I was a pretty wallflower then. And now the sun shines on me every day because I have my dolls with me.

I prefer the four bedroom walls that confine me to be myself... and to be with my dolls. Everyone on the outside doesn't get me. I often look out of my window to watch the other kids banter and play, and I pity them because they don't know the meaning of the word play. Play has to have an element of imagination in it. I imagine my dolls as being real friends. When they look at me, it feels as if they understand me better than I even understand myself. With them I am no longer alone. I am with true friends and I am grateful for that.

On the day that I became a woman, I wasn't locked in my bedroom all the time. When the party was over, I grabbed my dolls and went outside, to my playhouse in the backyard. I had five dolls with me in the playhouse that day: Tris, Matty, Larry, Arty & Matron.

Tris is a very cute doll. She has rosy red cheeks and a bunch of different ribbons, bows and outfits to wear. She tends to love everything and everybody.

Then there is Matty. He is a GI doll and he takes care of me and keeps me safe. He dodged the Falklands war draft.

Larry is actually a teddy bear, but he's such a doll. He has teeth and he has the appetite of a grown man. All the girls are crazy about him.

Arty is also not a doll, though he (like Larry) is one to me. He's a stuffed owl. He goes 'too-wit-too-woo' when you press his tummy. He's smart, wise even, and gives me good advice. He also likes to whisper, so it's sometimes hard to hear what he's trying to say.

Finally, there's my matron. Unlike Arty and Larry, she is actually a doll (like Matty and Tris). She's also a nurse. She even came with her own watch and thermometer. I see Matron as a sibling because she has a personality that really takes after my mother. She is usually kind to me and the others, but sometimes she can be a handful. I know she's just looking out for all of us, but she can hurt my feelings when she's being bossy.

Anyway, we are all together almost every day. They are the members of my own special clique and no one can separate us. We are best friends for life.

They helped me to solve the mystery of play and imagination. Playtime is a means used by parents to lock children in rooms of imagination so that the adults can play as well.

Case in point: my mother. When I was younger she would bring me a doll or take me to the playhouse whenever she had to smoke a cigarette in the front yard or when she wanted to drink herself to sleep in front of the television. She drinks a lot.

I think it's all society's fault. Society led my mother and the other adults to a dark place. That's because society needs to play too. It plays by watching all of us busy ourselves with objects, philosophies and ideas. Society is an observer, it's not here to mediate or solve any mysteries. It just wants to play forever.

Why is my mother so distant and drunk lately? I think I might have the answer: Billy changed her. She changed more and more to fit in with his way of thinking. And he is an asshole. I don't like him at all. Unlike Billy, my dolls never change and that's why I love them so much.

The foundations of this understanding fell into place on the day that I became a woman.

I decided right there and then that I would grow up. I would blend in as others have forced me to do and I would use it all to my advantage. I realised that there was tremendous power in invisibility. Since society wants to prolong the mystery of play, it won't perform experiments and derive a reaction from me. It won't try to figure me out.

I grew up because I have figured out society. Before that day, I longed to derive a reaction from it. I longed to experiment with society to come up with a different result. But the monotony of play was killing my imagination, my hold on mystery.

I needed to create a new philosophy.

I didn't come to this conclusion alone. My thoughts helped me. They were locked in the room with me, living in my dolls. My dolls became the embodiments of my raw subconscious. We debated for a long time. Debating with my dolls (my thoughts) has always been my rationale against my anxieties. The problem is that usually my anxieties win.

My dream is that one day I will have enough money to move away. Especially from Billy. I would get my own place, and each of my best doll friends would have their own room.

I'm speechless.

My first thought is that Destiny must be suffering greatly with her mental health, which is a notion I can relate to. I knew there was some kind of a problem but

I didn't think it was this bad. I also know that she shouldn't suffer by herself. She's still so young and fragile, and she doesn't know what's right for her. But she has one advantage I never had: a mother who cares. And one who always knows what's best for her child.

These are the facts: my daughter is lonely and her friends are dolls.

I have to get rid of those damn dolls so that she can go outside and meet some real friends, real *people*. Maybe, just maybe, she will then start to have fun like a normal person. But first I need to keep on reading. I need to keep on reading to get to the bottom of this resentment she is building up in her head against Billy.

Afraid of what is going to be revealed by the diary, I tuck it in underneath my arm and go to the kitchen to pour myself a glass of red wine. I need alcohol for this.

Once I've taken a deep swig of Merlot, I continue to read

Over the years I've developed my own coping mechanisms. Most often it was silence, something that drove those who considered me a friend (or at least those who I spent time with) insane. They avoided me, but that was fine because I had my dolls to keep me company.

The same doesn't go for my mother though. Now that I'm older I have a yearning desire to get to know her better. Unfortunately, that's out of the question. She spends all her time with Billy now. He's taken her away from me and that's the second reason why I don't like him.

My low self-esteem is my third reason for disliking Billy. That flaw in me is also his fault. He overprotected me throughout my time in primary school. Sure, it was cool when I was younger, but by the time I reached my teenage years, the other kids would pick on me for having him looking out for me all the time. The issue I faced was that I became dependent on him and that he was my only real friend.

But teenage girls should have friends their own age, everybody told me.

I need to get rid of Billy. So perhaps if I never speak to him, he would get the message. Being passive-aggressive is maybe the best approach. And then my dolls can be my father figure. I don't need Billy. He's not even my real dad. No matter what he does and how he acts, he will never be anything like the loving father I deserved to have in my life.

I realise I'm a little out of breath. She is under some delusional impression that Billy is a bad influence on me. And I now recall that Destiny has told me before that I've been acting differently ever since I met him. The problem is that I was too ignorant to listen to her.

On top of everything she thinks that I have some sort of drinking problem, which is strange because I don't drink any more than the regulars who visit the pub down the road.

Billy is the real victim here, and it is totally unfair of Destiny to vilify him. She used to love him, but they grew further apart over the years and now she has built resentment toward him. I don't think any of this is Billy's fault. These are my daughter's issues, not his.

I consider her schooling. It is known for poor teaching and violence amongst the students. We've always tried to protect her from the bullies and physical violence but whenever we got involved in her life she told us, 'Don't get involved, it only perpetuates more bullying.'

That's not going to happen anymore. I will get involved from now on. I know what's best for my daughter — she's only a little girl after all.

When she was younger she would cry about the bullies and Billy, the football coach Billy, would cheer her up. Now that Destiny is in secondary school, she doesn't have him acting as her security guard and protecting her from all the bullies any longer.

I need to find out what the real issue here is.

First of all, I tell myself that I definitely don't have a drinking problem. I'm just a mum who likes having fun with the girls from the estate. What does Destiny expect? Should I sit in the house all day and drink tea while knitting jerseys? She's lucky she has a fun and outgoing mother. Sure, there are rare occasions when I come home drunk, but they are few and far between. I have a high tolerance for alcohol, so a drinking binge only just gets me a little tipsy.

I feel that after reading her diary, I know better what she needs. She needs precious bonding time, not only with me but also with Billy; especially with Billy. It will help her to be less alone and more comfortable with us. She should be able to tell us everything and I must urge her to do so. I was under the impression that she's my best friend and I'm hers. But instead, I've now learned that she's been telling me nothing about her troubled thoughts. I feel betrayed and angry. Apparently, to her, I know fuck-all about her life. My anger turns to frustration as I reflect on all the hard work I've put in raising her. What does she know about life? Nothing, that's what.

***

Two days later, I still feel guilty about reading Destiny's diary. Maybe the curse she's placed on me is real.

However, it can't be, because I don't believe in all of that witchcraft crap. Plus, I returned the diary to her room; it's not like I've stolen it or something. I do need to alleviate some of this guilt though, that's for sure.

I can't go on like this. It's nerve-racking and will get in the way of me caring for Destiny, but I also have my own mental health to consider. She should be more aware of that. So, I decide that it's the right thing to do to get it off my chest. Talking about our problems always works best, no matter what the scenario might be. I cannot allow anything to eat me up, because it will consume my entire life and I'll become a different person.

The issue I'm facing is that the only person I want to speak to about Destiny is Destiny, and she's the only one I can't speak to. The irony pains me. Anyway, I know Destiny very well and if I told her I read her diary, she would never speak to me again. I simply can't afford to be in the same situation I was in with my mother whilst growing up.

Wait, Billy can help. Together we can think of the best way to take care of this bloody mess. And I'm sure Billy will understand why I went through Destiny's diary. When he comes home, I use the same technique he used with me when breaking the news that Destiny had been skipping school. I sit him down at the kitchen table. My daughter is in her bedroom behind closed doors, listening to rock music.

'Billy,' I say, staring into his eyes. 'I read Destiny's diary.' I look down, ashamed.

'You did what?' he shouts back at me. I've seen this side of him before. He is fuming. He has completely lost his temper within a split-second.

'Calm down, please,' I plead.

Eventually he does. But it's worrying to see Billy get into this kind of state all the same. He is usually a very calm and relaxed person. But this revelation has hit him quite hard. His argument is that it was an invasion of privacy and that it was unjust to intrude into Destiny's life like that. Surprisingly, I agree with him. He's right, but life is too short to have regrets. When I express to him the details of my findings, his sympathy for Destiny lessens.

The rest of the discussion provides me with some priceless information and a blueprint on how to fix things. We agree that I need to get rid of her stupid dolls and that Billy needs to form a closer bond with my daughter. So, I organise for Billy to take Destiny out on a trip to somewhere nice. Someplace where he can really spend the day treating and spoiling her. It's a master plan. Not only will the pair of them have precious bonding time, but I will have the opportunity to go into her room and destroy all her dolls. It will be a sacrifice for the greater good. It's part of being a good mother.

The plan goes ahead. I wave goodbye to the two of them as they drive off. Destiny sits impatiently in the passenger seat. I can tell she's agitated, but mother knows what's best.

I execute my side of the plan well, but Billy fails miserably on his end. He takes her to Canary Wharf, the urban business district in the wealthy eastern part of London. If you give someone a taste of a different way of life, they leech on to it. It's like a seed being planted. Although, to be honest with myself, it is partially my fault. They left before I could even ask what their destination was. I've trusted Billy while my mind was elsewhere. I was so focussed on destroying Destiny's dolls (and worrying about how she might react when she found out) that I never concentrated on the trip they were taking.

Destiny comes home with a smile I haven't seen on her face for years. She approaches me and says, 'Thank you for arranging the trip to London, Mummy.'

I hold her in my arms and reply, 'How was it, darling?'

Destiny responds with, 'I'm happy now, Mum. I saw the rich people and how delighted they are, and I want to be one of them.'

I immediately get annoyed. 'Shut your fucking mouth,' I tell her, yanking her ear hard. 'You're an ungrateful little sod, that's what you are.' I send her off to her room. As she walks out of the living room, tail between her legs, I realise that my reaction was more of a reflex than a reaction, simply because I won't allow Destiny to speak about wealthy people like that. But she's still my daughter, and I know if I make a big deal out of this, it will become her mission to try and prove me wrong, and all she'll think about is money and materialism.

I call her back, embrace her and apologize. I promise her that I will never swear at her like that again. She continues to shed tears. They're happy tears, I figure.

But then wriggles herself loose from my hug and runs to her bedroom. When she enters, she slams the door shut and screams, 'I hate you, bitch!'

The dolls. I hate myself.

Chapter 9

The Jolly Goat

My life is far from paradise.

Things are (and have been recently) rather difficult. I want Destiny to become the strongest young woman she can possibly be and if that means her being mad at me all the time, then I'm really okay with it. We are also struggling to pay the bills and I feel guilty that Billy had to take up a second job at our local supermarket.

It's time to take action. I decide to get a job.

Congratulations to me. I have always had the selfish attitude that I will only work as long as I genuinely enjoy it. However, that was when I didn't need the money. Now I do.

I've been forging a much closer friendship with Strawberry during my many visits to the Jolly Goat pub and grill. Our conversations have opened new metaphorical doors for me to walk through, as well as one real door — the door to the pub. She talks to the manager and he offers me a position as a second bartender, reporting to Strawberry. I take the job. How difficult can it be to pour a pint instead of drinking one?

I start a week later and I soon realise that I enjoy working at the Jolly Goat.

Within a couple of weekends, I become a big name in Lansbury. I'm the bartending lady with the quick and diligent hands. It means a lot to me. There isn't a person on the estate who doesn't know Brenda Allen. I feel a part of something really special.

Since Destiny's birth and up until now, my life has been about her. Now I owe it to myself to pursue my own passion, something that will give me a bit of a break and the breathing space I've been craving. I'm literally not qualified to do anything — or at least that's what I always thought — but I find myself having a real knack for pouring pints of beer.

***

Three months later, life is treating me better for a change.

It's Destiny's thirteenth birthday. The look on her face when Billy comes home with a caterpillar cake is priceless.

I feel a little sad though. My relationship with Strawberry has begun to go in the wrong direction. I love my job, but Strawberry used to be a much better friend than she is now a boss. This is teaching me a valuable lesson: to anyone who wants to maintain a positive, healthy and sustainable friendship with someone else, never work with them. I mean, it is like Strawberry becomes a different person as soon as she puts on the head-bartender uniform. The environment completely changes her. She becomes this monster as soon as she steps into the Jolly Goat. She is rude, nasty and, worst of all, whiny. It isn't okay.

We do have a mutual professional respect toward one another, but deep down we are both becoming sick of each other. I feel as though I am always under surveillance when I'm at work. Strawberry expects too much of me and I have my own secret ways of coping. Whenever she's not at the Jolly Goat, I treat myself to bottomless beer on tap, chased by shots of whiskey. Billy also appreciates the free drinks when he comes to visit me at work.

Strawberry purposefully keeps on booking me for weekend shifts. Saturdays and Sundays are days I should be spending with Destiny to repair our mother-daughter relationship.

To handle all of this, I try to ease the pain by doing something else I haven't done since I was a child — I read. Similar to the experience of falling asleep and being reborn again in a dream, reading helps me block out reality. My mother used to force me to do a ton of reading while I grew up. I despised being forced to do so, but it gave me a fantastic opportunity to relax, nonetheless. Now that my life is consumed by long shifts and a busy schedule, I'm careful to make time for myself. Fiction novels, in particular, are great to read. They allow me to journey on a magical adventure in my head. Sometimes I need that.

I haven't done much reading during Destiny's hectic upbringing. Whenever I tried, I ended up telling myself that I was too busy or too tired. For years I've felt an element of guilt when trying to do the things that I love. But lately, I've started doing just that by reading books. It serves as a helpful relief from work stress. And this time I make a transition from the epic adventure tales I've read when I was younger to reading mothercare self-help books. I am hesitant at first, because I know I can become obsessed with certain things and if I'm not cautious, it can dominate my life.

All this aside, I forge on and dive into the mothercare books. They end up leading me down an interesting path and I eventually stumble upon something that has the possibility to change my life. I find a book to assist in framing my mentality and emotional well-being. As humans we are always growing and developing. We are all flawed and we constantly need to try to improve ourselves. This book becomes my treasure chest.

It is called *So, you want to be the best possible mother or the best possible person?* and it teaches me that looking after myself is just as important (if not more important) as looking after my child. It speaks a lot about how many mothers lose their identities while trying to raise children. They often make sacrifices like quitting their jobs or giving up their hobbies. My life right now has been revolving around taking care of my beautiful daughter and catering to her every need. I am incredibly inspired by what I read in my treasure chest. I decide that it is time to write a new chapter in my own life's book.

It comes as a sparkling idea, one of those sudden light bulb moments from out of nowhere. I think back to the time when I took Destiny to the nursery for the first time. Those mothers had the classic Lansbury aesthetic. My frame of mind is also supplemented by still seeing pictures of all those mothers on social media. They seem so happy and I now know that I can be like them, too. I'm not feeling self-conscious about my looks anymore. That is something of the past. No more will I glare at myself in the mirror and see a reflection of my sad past. Brenda is a new woman and she is living her best life. I decide to start planning for something significant, something that will change not only my life, but also Billy's.

I awake one morning with blurry eyes. I rub away the sleep, then roll over and look at my gorgeous boyfriend. He is all I ever wanted. I'm so fortunate and today I'm going to make him a lucky man. I have something important to tell him, but I need to wait for the appropriate moment. My timing has to be perfect.

Going down to the kitchen, I prepare my coffee, pour a bottle of beer into a tall glass and light a cigarette. It is a combination I like to call the triple threat, a perfect *ménage à trois* to kick-start my morning properly. I feel stimulated by the caffeine and the nicotine rush, whilst the beer acts as a depressant, keeping me composed and level-headed.

Life is beautiful, except for the fact that the Jolly Goat is going to be rather busy tonight — it's Saturday. Every morning around this time I get a phone call from Strawberry regarding my shifts. She always makes me work on Saturday nights. When I answer my phone she says, 'You're working afternoon and evening shift. I need you tonight. Make sure you are there, girl.' While this is not a surprise, I'm sort of gutted. I was hopeful because I wanted to do something nice with Billy tonight. I figured we might go to the Chinese restaurant up the road. The chef, Wong Chu, makes the best chow mein in the world.

Hours pass. I relax on the couch in the living room, watching the television, until I receive a text message. It's from Strawberry

Hi Brends, got a big favour to ask ya acts, I'm gonna need you to manage the pub tonight. I ain't gonna be there coz I'm ill. Rly soz. Hope that's K, Thnks.

I respond with a *'K'* and smile at my phone.

The first thing that comes to mind is, *Thank goodness, I don't have a spy watching over my shoulder while I'm at work tonight.* I close my eyes and play out two separate scenarios.

One part of me — the responsible side that thinks I have to be a thoughtful and trusted employee — suggests that I should look after the establishment and do my job professionally. The other — the more erratic and careless side of me — tells me that I owe it to myself to take full advantage of the situation. I finally go with this latter scenario.

I now know that tonight is the perfect opportunity to tell Billy my good news, while I also get a chance to treat him. He has been working so hard at school lately, poor thing.

I go upstairs where he is still in bed, reading yesterday's paper. He looks up at me and says, 'You alright, darling?'

'Better than alright, love' I reply enthusiastically. 'Billy, please be at the Jolly Goat tonight.' I turn and then, as I leave the room and close the door, I add, 'Oh, and bring all the lads with you, I've got a surprise for you all.'

There, my plan is in motion. I'll sort them all out with free drinks and then I will make my special announcement in front of everyone. It will be a perfect night and a great gift to Billy. With only him and his friends there, my job will be particularly easy tonight. All I have to do is change the open sign in the window to closed and no one would disturb my private party.

***

The time comes and I flip the sign. It's already dark outside.

An hour later (and three double whiskeys stronger) I am ready to announce my surprise. The waitresses don't really understand why we are so empty. I feel sorry for them, since they won't be earning any tips tonight. Hence, I have them sit down at the biggest table in the pub and set them up with bottomless beer.

'Everyone,' I call out from behind the bar counter. 'I have an announcement to make.'

Billy stands up and interrupts. 'Before you say anything, sweetheart, I want to tell all the lads that came here how lucky I am to have a gem like you in my life. Thank you for tonight, babe. I love you loads.'

'That was beautiful,' I say nervously. 'Which is why I have something for you, Billy.'

'*And* she has something for me,' Billy jests, chuckling while looking at his friends. 'What else could I possibly want? I have everything I need right here.'

'Aww,' I respond. 'Billy.'

The men in the pub begin to pound their palms on the tables, making drumroll sounds.

I gaze at my boyfriend and say, 'Billy, your beautiful girlfriend has made an investment in herself yesterday. You'll be happy to know she is getting her breasts enlarged. You will be even happier to know that she's already paid for the surgery herself.'

The lads all smile and then start cheering. They all love to applaud and whistle, especially in moments like this one. Billy's two best friends grab him by the shoulders and lift him up, while continuing to shout. He looks uncomfortable, which is uncharacteristic. His jaw has dropped and the expression on his face is that of confusion and utter shock.

I don't quite understand. Why would he be upset about this? Not only am I the best mother, but now I'm also the best girlfriend, surely. Isn't that what every guy wants? Billy should be over the moon. I ask him why he is acting so strange and he tells me it's nothing, he's only stressed about the upcoming interschool football tournament.

For the rest of the night, he seems off. He won't acknowledge my presence and he avoids the glances I give him from behind the bar counter. Although he does put on a brave face as he tries to have fun with his friends. He doesn't want to be the party-pooper, I guess.

When we return home from the pub, shortly before midnight, my phone is constantly vibrating with incoming calls from Strawberry. I don't answer any of them.

As soon as we enter the house, the look in Billy's eyes says it all; he is absolutely fuming. Destiny is still awake, listening to music on the carpet in the living room.

After I've eased the door shut, Billy begins an argument but I cut him off. 'I don't want to do this in front of Destiny,' I tell him in my firmest voice.

'Well, I've got nothing to hide, so let's talk about this right here, right now.' He pauses for a moment and then resumes. 'You complain about the difficulty of paying the bills, and now you're doing this?'

I stutter. I can't come up with a suitable response.

Before I can tell Destiny to go to her room, Billy asks, 'Why are you being so secretive with me, woman?' Anguish is written all over his forehead. 'Where did you get the money from? And you better tell me the truth.' He steps closer to me and I feel rather intimidated by him for the first time ever.

I shudder. I can't possibly tell him that I have millions of Pounds hidden inside a massive mansion. So, I refuse to say anything. I keep my mouth sealed.

'So, now you're not going to speak?' he shouts. 'Last chance,' he whispers through gritted teeth, as his face turns bright red. The thick blue vein on the side of his head is pulsating. Billy winds back his arm and he swings it at my face.

I hit the floor with a bang.

All I can see is black.

I scream in a loud, high-pitched tone while curling my body up into a ball. My hands can't stop shaking.

Billy is standing over me. I look up in time to see a tear dropping from beneath his right eye. His breathing pace increases to the point of hyperventilation. He gasps for air.

It is at this point that I start thinking about my childhood. Specifically, my mind wanders back to the story I told Professor Rupert Williams all those years ago. The story of the day my father became possessed and thought I was a demon. That was the only other time someone has hurt me in the past. Physical hurt, that is. Not the emotional and mental hurt my mother has inflicted on me throughout my life.

My current situation takes me back to those darker days.

Days I've assumed were in the past.

Chapter 10

What Have I Become?

Moments after Billy has hit me, I collapse onto the sofa mattress in our living room.

He has stormed off and locked himself in the master bedroom, the one that we've shared for several years now. Destiny is nothing short of hysterical. She has also gone to her bedroom and her cries can most likely be heard from miles away. I figure it is probably best to leave her alone. She will eventually cry herself to sleep.

The alcohol in my system is masking the pain somewhat, but I need to do something about the swelling. I push myself up and drag my feet to the kitchen. We don't have ice, so I hold a packet of frozen peas against my face while sobbing like a baby. It feels like I'm living in a nightmare. Our house is all of a sudden filled with negative energy. For the first time since my childhood, I really sense the broken family syndrome again, except this time it is a family that I am mothering, not the evil Betty Allen. And I can't stand it. I feel like a bloody failure. But deep down I know I'm not. I can't be. I'm nothing like my mother and I never will be.

On a normal night, red wine is my poison of choice during these late hours. Just the right amount tends to get me drowsy enough to sleep. It usually works like magic. I just sip on the precious scarlet nectar and all of my problems magically go away.

Tonight is different, though, and desperate times call for desperate measures. I whip out the big gun: supermarket-brand vodka in a plastic bottle. This shit burns like fire on the way down, I know that from experience. Not even the Russians can handle it. I unscrew the cap and bring the bottle to my lips before gulping down a good four shots. It hits hard but it's comforting. I screw the cap back on and throw the bottle down to the floor. It bounces like a rubber ball.

I suck in a breath of air and then stare up at the dirty, cracked ceiling. Everything around me is spinning like a carousel. I close my eyes but the room is still spinning. I wish somebody could pull me out of this sick nightmare.

Once I've regained my composure I go into the spare bedroom. Billy is still in our room and the door is still locked. I remove my earrings and place them on the nightstand. I put my mobile phone down next to them. My mind is in disarray, so I light some incense sticks to try and relax. They tend to calm me down in situations like these. At the very least, they will make the smell of cigarette smoke and mildew go away.

I lie down and study the single light bulb hanging above the bed for a while. Then my eyes shift to the wall and I can't help but feel discomforted by the spiderwebs in the corner of the room. I get up to get rid of them and I catch a glimpse of myself in the dressing table's mirror.

I freeze and take a long, hard look at myself. My dress is covered in yellow whiskey stains and I look like a drunken mess. For a second, the thought of whether I am actually proud of who I really am flashes through my mind. I squeeze my medium-sized boobs with both hands, imagining what they would look like after the surgery.

Then I snap back to the present. I need to escape this reality. It reminds me too much of the recurring vivid nightmares I've been having lately. These night terrors are without exception flashbacks to my childhood; imagery of my past that I constantly suppress in my conscious state. Perhaps the dreams are a direct reflection of my life, who knows? I force my eyes closed and start humming my favourite song, the one that is already on replay in my head.

Nothing in life is certain, except for my sleep deprivation. Nightmares are a phenomenon so unexplainable to me, yet fully a part of my life. Some people say the origin of nightmares has implications of an inexplicable evolutionary response to danger, that they prepare us for future reality and teach us lessons about past reality. I've also heard that nightmares can consist of literally anything our imagination can create. My nightmares are a reflection of my presence in my past. My subconscious is trying to release itself. I am haunted by myself. I try to forget about my past as much as I can, in order to focus on the present.

I shake my head, switch off the light and then zombie-walk back to the bed to lie down once more, having completely forgotten about the cobwebs. I climb in without undressing. My mind is too weary to concentrate on such a simple task.

After countless hours with my eyes wide shut, I eventually fall asleep.

The dreams begin instantly — lucid and vibrant, in bright colours and with pinpoint detail. It feels like I have just walked out of a time machine. Distinguishing between reality and my dreams becomes impossible. I have no control over my subconscious. I'm seeing the parts of my past that remind me of the present day. I'm trying to eradicate my past, but I live in it again.

What's even worse is that it's against my will.

Apparently nightmares haven't heard of the word consent.

Chapter 11

My Childhood Haunts Me

My mother is shouting at me, telling me that I will never be good at anything.

She is a shriveled old hag. I try to yell back, but I cannot find my voice — the same as when I was younger. Betty is racing toward me with a cricket bat in her liver-spot covered hands, ready to take my head off.

As she swings the bat, I wake up. Waking up is as bad as the nightmare. The sun is shining through the half-open curtains and I'm hung over as hell. It takes me a few moments to realise that I'm not in our room but, in fact, in the spare bedroom.

I feel as if I was hit by a ton of bricks in my sleep. Reality should be like a waft of fresh air, but it isn't. Reality is pain. My mouth is as dry as a desert and I have a headache straight from the devil's stare. I'm also in a state of panic. It comes over me like sleep paralysis. I can't move any of my muscles. The sickening nightmare continues to loop around relentlessly in my mind. I can't control it. This nightmare is the worst one I've had in a long while. It takes me back to a time in my life when I struggled, a time in my life I thought was over for good. No matter how hard anyone tries, memories simply can't be erased. I guess that certain moments, even if they seem to be over, still last forever in our subconscious. The past… it isn't only our history, it is also sometimes manifesting as our living present.

The first actionable thought that comes to mind is that I need to do something about my sanity, anything, as soon as I can. It's my body and my mind's way of telling me that things are very wrong and I'm not someone to ignore a clear sign when it's right in front of me.

I think back and recall that the last time my mental health has deteriorated this badly was many years ago, when I was still pregnant with Destiny. I sought professional treatment back then, and it was totally useless because I fell in love with the shrink, except for the fact that it actually cured me, so in that sense, it did work.

But I don't want to go back because I'm too self-conscious. On the other hand, I think that sometimes, no matter how strong you feel you are, you have to accept defeat.

I ultimately concede and decide to go back to therapy. I am so desperate and when you're desperate you make erratic decisions. In moments like these we act on impulse, rather than thinking clearly. It's a case of the evolutionary parts of our human nature surfacing and encouraging us to follow these impulses rather than thinking rationally and with clear logic.

I climb out of bed and fetch my mobile phone from the nightstand, then give the handsome Dr. Rupert Williams a call. He answers after the second ring. I suppose he doesn't have caller-ID activated. He greets me as a stranger and, without telling him who I am and with a slight tremble in my voice, I say, 'I had a vicious nightmare.'

'Oh,' he responds.

It doesn't help much. I think he knows it's me. He must have recognised my voice.

'Why bother calling?' he asks, which is a fair question, I guess.

I assume he thinks I will be coming to his practice regardless of my phone call. It's unfair to make assumptions about people, though, especially when you don't know them well enough and you haven't spoken to them in years. Unfortunately, though, his assumption is right on the money. Maybe I haven't changed after all.

Anyway, I can tell that he isn't very enthusiastic about hearing from me. It is easy to gauge that from his irritated tone of voice. However, bearing in mind the fact that I haven't seen him and his wife since Destiny's birth, I think it's pretty safe to say that enough time has passed now to see him in person once again. I mean, it seems socially acceptable. He can console me about my problems once more. Plus, another point — I can't stress this point enough — it is his *duty* to care for people with mental health issues. He can't possibly refuse a patient. That would be a PR nightmare, worse than mine from last night. I know he wouldn't want to go down that route, especially not with me, given that historic event in the glasshouse more than a decade ago.

There is one more decisive factor that stands out most of all, and this is the one that can't really be ignored. It is the very reason why I want to go back to Dr. Rupert Williams instead of any other therapist. I feel like he is still the only one I can trust with my emotions. He is the only one who can truly understand me. He knows my dark, secret past. He knows about my angels, devils and demons. He knows, more than I do, how impossibly weak I am in the face of my failures. I ask him for a face-to-face consultation and he reluctantly agrees to see me.

***

I sit in front of him, hopefully for the last time in my life. His thinning hair has turned grey since our encounter in his house on that dreadful morning.

After clearing my throat, I begin. 'Dr. Williams, at the time I felt so old and wise beyond my years, but in reality I was so young. And, like most children, I was also quite impressionable. Let's just say I felt kind of conflicted. In many ways I thought I was in charge of the world, when in reality the world was in charge of me. I was a cute and innocent little girl who was being corrupted by everything and everyone around her. At the time I asked myself, "Why did they corrupt her like that? She shouldn't be at fault here. She simply didn't know any other way of life." This was what I used to think. In my head, I genuinely believed that every other child all around the world lived in the same way I did. That's how naïve I was.

'But in a way, it makes sense. When you're that young, you can't see the bigger picture. You become isolated. When you are confined exclusively by your household environment, you lack a point of reference for other ways of life. I think that is why cults are so successful. They manage to exclude you from life outside of the cult. They often prey on the souls of innocent and naïve people. They suck vulnerable people in like a vacuum cleaner. My mother was such a vacuum cleaner. It was psychologically damaging, even more so because of my lack of awareness. I was also trapped by a large-scale, class-based social alliance that confined its members until they gained knowledge. At some point I argued that if that was what life would be forever, then the game wasn't really for me. Which is why I constantly felt unhappy, even at such a young age. But I didn't have enough knowledge back then. It was a sadness without reason.'

I am speaking so rapidly that I can't quite compartmentalise my thoughts properly.

'Slow down,' Dr. Williams tells me, as if reading my mind. 'Take some deep breaths.'

I do as I'm told.

He nods and then says, 'I'm going to require you to explain every detail about your nightmare, but first you're going to have to talk to me properly. This will involve you giving me a little background information. So please, start by telling me about your upbringing.'

'Well,' I begin. 'I grew up in a small community in a traditional British settlement. The area is called Radlett. Whenever my parents were asked to describe where we lived, they would say that it was in an affluent village situated in a county called Hertfordshire, north of London's borders. The place is widely considered upmarket with a small population. Anyway, our house was on a private estate, secluded and closed off from the rest of the village. The fences surrounding our property separated me from the outside world. But it was in a gorgeous countryside, filled with stunningly beautiful forests. If you see the picturesque landscape, you would think that I would grow up to be the happiest person in the world.'

I pause for a moment, catching my breath, then continue.

'I think for you to understand my childhood, you need to know about Charles Allen, my father, or my ex-father as I now call him. He was a light in my life during the early years. A real inspiration, if you will. He retired at the age of twenty-five, after selling the recruitment company that was handed down to him by his father. I never knew my grandpa. He died young — most likely lung cancer from smoking too much. Actually, I'm pretty sure of this because my father said he picked up the filthy habit from his dad. The millions of Pounds weren't the only thing he inherited from his father. Anyway, throughout my dad's life, it's safe to say that he did pretty well for himself. That is if you're foolish enough to judge success by one's financial stability in a socially constructed hierarchy.

'My father doted on me from a very young age. From as early as I can remember, he was always praising my long brown hair and my big brown eyes. Every evening, after reading the newspaper, smoking his cigar and drinking his coffee, he would spend hours telling me fantastic stories. After the first three or four, I would pretend to fall asleep. Then he would sing softly in my ear and gently caress my face. Wait, I'm missing something here… Oh, yes, before the story telling, he would look out the window and draw the curtains closed. Before that even, I would hear his reassuring footsteps coming down the hallway, from his study to my bedroom. He would tell me to be a good girl, to be respectful to my peers, and to brush my hair each morning with the jade hairbrush he gave me for my fifth birthday. That was our evening ritual.

'During the days, Daddy used to spend pretty much all of his time at the Radlett golf club. His "home away from home" as he liked to call it. "Honey, I'm not home." Those were the famous words my dad used to bellow out as he entered our front door. It was a running joke he had with my mother. He thought it was hilarious. She didn't. We loved to annoy her for some reason, both my father and I. Whenever we had the chance we would work on her nerves. My mother would be furious on the inside, but she always put on a faux relaxed face when Daddy wound her up. Looking back on it now, she was probably just holding it all in...'

I pause, trying to gather my thoughts once more.

'The golf club was all he ever really spoke about with enthusiasm, especially since my mother banned him from speaking about *her* around the house. She... she always used to question Daddy about Becky, his former personal assistant. Even when my dad retired from work, Becky still tended to accompany him — pretty much everywhere from as far as I can remember — much to the dismay of my mother. When she was still formally employed as his personal assistant, Becky would help him out with just about everything, even after hours. I don't know if he ever paid her for her overtime, but she often came to our house in the evenings. It was kind of weird, because there was nothing he actually needed help with. Yet, strangely enough, she would still hang out there. She was his best lady friend and maybe — now that I think about it — even closer to him than my mother had ever been. My dad had also known Becky longer than my mother. They were old school pals and used to date before he'd met my mother. Becky was even my dad's date to the high school prom. And he gave her the job as a favour. He would always try to reassure my mother that they were only friends, nothing more. However, when it came to discussing Becky, my father and mother simply didn't see eye to eye. But enough about Becky. Another thing my dad used to go on and on about was the fact that he had a V.I.P package at the club. I've said that right?'

'Yes,' the doctor replies. 'Go on.'

'I still recall how he used to speak about the perks at the club after a solid round of golf. He wouldn't stop talking about the top quality food and the fancy snacks like caviar and expensive olives, imported from Greece. Oh, and not to mention the "free" bottles of champagne that he so adored, along with many other luxuries. He must have paid a fortune for that V.I.P membership, but he made sure he got the most out of it. Dad was quite a heavy drinker, see?

'Of course, my mother loathed the way he entered the house staggering and slurring his words whenever he came home from the golf club. I remember this one time when she said to him, "Well, is it the alcohol or the drugs?" At that stage, I asked myself, "Why would the drugs make him behave like this?" I mean, I knew my mother always tried to remind my dad to take his prescription medication, but I never considered the possibility of him taking street drugs.

'Things got particularly bad one night when my mother secretly snooped around on Dad's phone while he was sleeping. She never really treated him the same after whatever she discovered that night. The final breaking point came when my mother decided to invite a special guest over for dinner. Mother used to be particularly close with Adrienne's dad. Adrienne was my best friend from school. I still remember how I thought their family was so cool because they were French. And what was even cooler was how my mother was best friends with her dad. Adrienne was going through a rough time because her parents had finalised their divorce. It was so nice that my mother cared so much and always wanted to console Adrienne's father, Antione. I loved how she and Antione used to get on so well.

'Anyway, the dinner parties my mother hosted were usually extravagant, especially when Antoine was invited. She would cover her face in tons of makeup and wear really stunning clothes at these dinner parties. There would always be flowers on the table, as well as several bottles of fine wine. It was all rather fancy. That was until my father decided to stumble home drunk with his arm around Becky's waist. As you can imagine, my mother wasn't too happy about that. And my dad was never quite the same after the incident.

'It was around the same time when Mother hired Aleksandra, our house cleaner. She did most of the chores in our home and she lived in the guest room in the eastern wing of the house. I was the only one who visited her room. It made sense, because my mother stopped mothering. And Aleksandra, well, she filled that void for me. After Aleksandra started working for us, Mother would cook fewer and fewer meals. As the days went by, she cared less and less for our family. Dad didn't help much, either. He was stretched out on the sofa almost every day, reading or watching the telly. He rarely ever moved. Yet, I was still surprised that he didn't say anything about my mother's blatant negligence. After a while, Dad started being exactly like my mother. He didn't care about anything anymore. It was almost as if the lethargy was a contagious disease in our household. Also, as my mother began to spend more time with Antione, my dad became like a zombie. I don't know how else to describe it. He was merely staring into nothingness, like those mentally unstable patients you see in the movies. I wasn't sure whether my mother and Antione getting closer to each other had anything to do with it though. I could have been coincidental timing. But, then again, it could have been because Dad became jealous of Antione. Mother said he was taking multi-vitamins to help keep him active, but I wasn't really sure what good it was doing. For someone taking that many vitamins, Dad should have been a lot healthier than he was, but he still hardly moved. He was simply going through the motions, as they say. He even stopped playing golf altogether. My father did nothing but rest all day, so inevitably I began to question what was wrong with him.

'There was a leisure centre near Radlett, in a town called Elstree. My mother would go there with Antione after they dropped us off at school. Even though Mother always wore her gym clothes — and so did Antoine — they never appeared to be getting any fitter. I was under the impression that they were sitting there, drinking iced coffee all day. Her friends, the other mothers from school, also used to meet them there. It made sense, as they were all free while their husbands were working. My mother called her group of friends her "gal pals."

'I'm assuming they would all gather together and gossip about the other parents in the school, but they would also go shopping together. Mother lived for the feeling of a credit card swipe. Coming back home with her arms full of shopping bags brought her tremendous pleasure. Daddy never questioned any of it. He left her to do whatever she wanted. And she got a taste of the good life, having all the money to use on whatever she desired. Quite honestly, I was always scared that they would get divorced because of the lack of time they actually spent together. Following Aleksandra's appointment, they even started sleeping in separate bedrooms. Come to think of it, the only time just the two of them would be in a room together is when they argued. They would go into one of the many bedrooms in the house, shout each other's ears off and half an hour later they would seem fine again. Whenever they argued, I locked myself in my room and listened to music… And that is about everything I recall from my childhood days. Everything before my father left us, that is. The nightmare I experienced took place in the time after his disappearance.'

Dr. Williams nods his head slowly. 'This is really interesting,' he says in a concerted manner. 'Now I want you to tell me about your nightmare.'

I swallow hard and then say, 'The dream took me back to an exceptionally tough time as a child. A time when I was so innocent and naïve, oblivious to the big world that surrounded me. Our past experiences develop us into the people we become, right? Well, this was an unpleasant experience, to say the least… My mother was shouting at me in the nightmare, telling me how I was no good. She was dripping with the ooze of cancer, and I was trying to yell back, but I couldn't find my voice. She has this damn cricket bat in her hands, ready to take my head off. She starts to swing, and then I wake up.

'I think we can all recall defining moments of our childhoods. One particular moment really stands out for me. It was about a year after my parents stopped sleeping in the same room. Suddenly, my dearest father left us. He was always resting anyway, so it was not too surprising to hear from my mother that he went somewhere to relax. To this day, I'm not sure where he went. Perhaps a meditation retreat or someplace similar. I tried not to ask too many questions. It was better that way, because I never liked the answers Mother gave me.

'As time went by I began to comprehend that my dad wasn't going to come back, that he had left us for good. At first I thought it was me, that I was the problem. I was a bad daughter, so he didn't care much about leaving me without a father. When I spoke to Aleksandra about it, she said that it was best for all of us. "Daddy is tightly wound," she told me. "And it's nobody but your mum's fault."

'My mother completely lost the plot after Dad had left. Aleksandra and I suffered heavily, since she would take her pain out on us. It wasn't really fair.

'On one occasion I forgot to take out the rubbish and my mother made me use my room as a dump for a whole week. Aleksandra intervened, though. She would come in at night and substitute the bags of trash with refuse bags filled with shredded newspaper. She sympathised with the torturous smell I had to endure. My mother only cared about trying to prove a point.

'The police asked me and my mother a few questions about my dad's "disappearance" but neither of us knew anything about it. Aleksandra insisted to speak to the police numerous times, but my mother would never allow her. The thought of Dad's disappearance obviously distressed me considerably. I would go up to my room and read books to distract myself from thinking too much about it. I loved reading when I was a child. It would distract me from reality. From the moment I buried my head in a new book, I would be unavailable to the world. No one would see me for days on end. Especially during the summer months between school terms.

'Dad went away on his own accord, my mother told me over breakfast, on one of the rare occasions that she actually cooked food. She prepared a proper English breakfast that day: eggs, bacon, toast with jam, and tea. She said that my father (and her former beloved husband) was troubled in his brain. She told me that she'd tried everything she could do to help him, paying ludicrous amounts of money to mental experts, to no avail. She thought it was time for him to be with himself, to reset and find peace of mind. I continued to miss my father for quite a long time. I mentioned him to my mother and she tried to ignore it, but when I asked about him a second time, a week later, she said he's doing great and then told me to leave it alone. But I kept on hoping that he could come back to us. I kept up the faith, you know?'

Dr. Williams looks at me, unblinking. 'And what other feelings did you have at the time?'

'Do you remember when I told you all those years ago about my father mistaking me for a demon?' I ask him.

'How could I forget?' he replies. There is sympathy in his eyes.

I sigh helplessly. 'After that happened, I tried to block it out. I've spent my whole life doing so. In fact… you're the first person I ever even told about it. I was too embarrassed. And I get flashbacks about it all the time. In my dreams, in my memories, in my subconscious, it's always there in the back of my mind.

'For a while, I thought my dad was right and that I really was a demon. It felt like something transcendent was taking over, inhabiting my mind and my body. I wasn't myself anymore. I couldn't think clearly and I couldn't enjoy all the things I enjoyed before my father's departure. My mother used to tell me that I was batshit crazy. She probably thought I had post-traumatic stress disorder. And she was most likely right. When I explained to her that the evil spirits have entered my soul, she became increasingly frustrated with me. She would call me a "schizophrenic" and tell me that I'm "becoming Charles," and that hurt me.'

There is a long, awkward moment of silence. Dr. Williams appears to be somewhat concerned. He has one eyebrow raised and his mouth is twitching. He stumbles his way through his words until he finds his composure and manages to say, 'I can imagine that was a tough time in your life. So, let me ask you this: what was the turning point for you? What helped you to get out of the rut you found yourself in?'

'Well… that happened around three years after my father had left. Life had become very uniform for me by then. I was like a soldier. "Good morning, Victoria," were the first words I would hear every morning. Words I don't recall ever hearing from my mother. She slept in a different section of the house so I didn't tend to bump into her before school. The "Good morning, Victoria," well, it had a slight Polish twang in the pronunciation of the words, something I actually enjoyed waking up to every morning. Our house cleaner would always greet me in a calm and soothing tone. So I developed a positive association with her voice. Aleksandra was originally from Gdańsk in Poland and she was great. She was like a mum to me in every way my birth mother wasn't. I was her life and her job was more than just a job for her. She cared so much about me. She used to pray for me all the time, and, the way she put it, she wanted to save my life. At the time I didn't quite understand what she meant by that, but looking back now, it all makes sense.

'My daily routine was monotonous and miserable. I wasn't alone, however, all the other kids at school hated their lives too. But I kept asking myself at the time, "How can I complain?" I thought I had every earthly possession a girl could ever want and more. Every morning Aleksandra would lay out my clothes for the day in a particular way that I've become accustomed to. It was always folded so beautifully and smelled like wild flowers. I still don't know where that smell came from, but I guess she must have used a scented talcum powder or something to that effect. Anyway, she would always have everything prepared perfectly, ensuring that my day would turn out the best it could. I loved her so much for that, and everything else she did for me. Yet, I found it really hard to express my feelings at times. This was because I often felt down in the dumps. I couldn't really explain why, but I wasn't happy. It was a deep-down inner pain that I just couldn't shake off. No matter what I did or how much I tried to push it from my mind, it simply wouldn't go away. And I didn't want to seem ungrateful to our house cleaner, so I forced myself to smile on a daily basis. I never even told her how much I appreciated her, but I'm sure she knew it.

'I was also under the impression that everyone my age felt the same pain I was feeling. But the other kids were much better than I was at putting on a fake smile. I just assumed that as soon as they had some alone time they would also weep and sob until their eyes were red and weary. Therefore, I admired their bravery and that even motivated me to be a stronger person.

'Aleksandra's house tasks always came with strict instructions from my mother. I felt sorry for her whenever she stepped out of line. I recall a day when my mother asked Aleksandra to wash the dishes and she broke one of the materialistic Betty Allen's beloved fine china plates. Mother could have replaced the plate with no problem at all, but to make a point she deducted the money from Aleksandra's wages and yelled in her face, "Do I have to fire you! I could get a chimpanzee to do your job. A bleeding chimp could do it, I swear!" I heard Antoine, Andrienne's dad, shout from upstairs, "What is that noise?" He was upstairs in his home office. He would work remotely on the computer from our house. My mother set this all up for him. He came downstairs, nostrils flaring, and spat a mouthful of coffee on the floor, then went back upstairs with the parting words, "Tell what's-her-face to clean up this mess." After that incident, Aleksandra felt as though she was treading on eggshells around my mother. She basically turned into a robot. She lacked emotion around me and she acted scared. Aleksandra would make phone calls to her family back home in Poland on Fridays. She would always refer to my mother as "Betty Bestia," but I knew this wasn't a compliment; it was said sarcastically.

'Each morning, when I was dressed and ready for the school day, Aleksandra would start her car's engine and pull up to the driveway in front of our house. This was always a struggle for her because she had a really old car. It was one of those bangers that seemed as if it could explode at any moment. She would roll down the window and call out my name. She wouldn't want to face the consequences of me being late for school, you know, because I would miss out on valuable learning time. It was *definitely not* because my mother would rip her head off and send it back to Gdańsk by first class delivery with the national mail.

'Anyway, whenever I saw her car, I always found it very strange that she couldn't afford something a little nicer, like my mother's car. I was so dumb and ignorant at the time. I thought that it was unfair for certain people to be rich and others, like Aleksandra, to be poor. Especially considering the fact that she definitely worked much harder than my mother did. "Surely she must be able to afford the same luxuries," I told myself. "Why would my mother, who does nothing all day, deserve a nicer car than her?" I asked Aleksandra one day why she didn't invest in a better, more reliable car. She only chuckled and brushed off the question. Perhaps she was saving for something else, or maybe she simply didn't like fancy, shiny automobiles as much as Mother and Antione did.

'On the way to school, we used to laugh and joke about my mother and how she acted around the house. At least, I sincerely hoped that most of the stuff Aleksandra said was meant in jest. She wasn't just our house cleaner and Betty Allen's personal slave, she was also my best friend. She was someone I could talk to about anything because she was always there for me, no matter what. Even though she was getting paid for it.

'Upon our arrival at the school, most children would have either both or one of their parents dropping them off. Their parents would give them hugs and kisses and tell them to have a wonderful day. I remember really wanting Aleksandra to kiss me or show me some sort of affection, but she always felt way too uncomfortable to do so. That affection barrier couldn't be crossed by her. Okay, so no one would kiss me goodbye in the morning, but at least I had a person that cared for me somewhat like a mum, which was all I could really ask for.

'During my school years, I always had a bit of trouble fitting in. The teachers spoke exactly like my mother did, and nothing like Aleksandra. They were also very different from Aleksandra because they didn't like having fun or playing games. I felt that they didn't care about us the way they should have. Aleksandra had a job, but she also cared — these teachers just had jobs. They were simply there to guide and facilitate our academic learning process, not to teach us social skills or how to deal with our emotions. So, of course, I hated them. Another issue was that they had such high expectations of us. I never felt as if I was good enough in school. Everyone in my class was excelling, while I wasn't making a lot of progress. I guess I didn't handle the pressure as well as they did.

'We were forced to do class-based reading every afternoon. That was the scariest part of my day. I had to read in front of all my friends, which would sound like a breeze to most people, but I was socially awkward and — although I loved reading alone in my bedroom — I wasn't very fluent when I had to read out loud. If this wasn't bad enough, I also had a really bad lisp when I was young, further reducing my confidence. Under pressure, my lisp would get worse, eventually transforming into stuttering. My face would go a bright red and I would feel as though I'm drowning, gasping for air while reading. I felt as if everyone was judging me while I was busy reading my part. I often got distracted and lost my place when I heard muttering and giggling from everyone in my class. Whenever I slipped up and made a mistake, they would relish the opportunity to mock me. The only girl in my class that actually cared about me was Andrienne. Perhaps I just liked people with cool accents, but Adrienne was my other best friend, after Aleksandra. Since she also struggled with family issues, we could relate to one another. Her's seemed much worse than mine, though. After her mother had divorced her father, Antione, they — Adrienne and her mum — moved into a smaller apartment outside the estate. Like me, Adrienne was sad all the time.

'Regardless of all the problems I faced, I tried to stay positive through it all at school. Aleksandra used to tell me all the time that every kid in my class loved me, even if they were showing it in mysterious ways. I can't say that I ever really felt that so-called love, but I had no reason to believe that Aleksandra would lie to me, so I just tried to get along with everyone around me. I mean, I could only try my best to be myself and hope for the best, right? And if they liked me for it, then that was going to be great. If not, I'd have to deal with it. And that's what I did. In the end I didn't connect with anyone at all, other than Adrienne. During breaks at school, I would take my lunchbox and walk outside to run around and play games after eating my sandwiches. I loved hopscotch, but the other kids wouldn't play nice with me. They were all so self-entitled and simply didn't wait their turn. This resulted in me giving up on even trying to fit in. So I would spend my free time just sitting on the benches behind the bus stop, sulking.

'After school was finished, our class would sit on the carpet in the hall's lobby as the various responsible adults came to pick us up. I was always the first one out, which made me really happy. Aleksandra would peek in through the door and wink at me. However embarrassing this was, I didn't care. She was the only authorised guardian on the school's list who was allowed to pick me up and she did, every day, without fail. I wished back then that one day I would be a parent and I promised myself that I would be the one to pick my kid up from school and see the smile on their face when I arrive. I also said a little prayer every day after school, hoping that my mother would surprise me by picking me up. Unfortunately, that was false hope. It never happened, not once.

'One of the other defining moments that changed my life actually happened while Aleksandra and I were doing something as uneventful as driving back home from school in her scrappy old car. She was always telling me about her friends and family who lived in Poland. She couldn't stop speaking about them; to the point where I felt as if I knew them as my own extended family. So, it was quite surprising when we were driving back home one afternoon in the winter and she told me about a "special best friend" she had here in England. That just happened to slip out during our casual conversation, like it was no big deal. It was a little uncharacteristic, because she seemed so secretive about him and we were normally very open with each other about everything. Before that day, she had never mentioned any friends here in the UK, only people in Poland. This guy's name was Steve and I was so excited for Aleksandra because when she spoke about him, her eyes glistened and a naughty smile played across her lips. I instantly suspected that she was a bit closer to Steve than she was pretending to be. So I wanted to dig deeper, and like a detective, it became my mission to find out more about the mysterious Steve.

'Aleksandra told me that he lived in Borehamwood. "Borehamwood?" I asked her. "Where on earth is that?" I was super curious as you can imagine. She told me that the place was actually not too far from Radlett. Then I recalled hearing the name before, that my mother had mentioned Borehamwood was full of peasants and that we should never go there because it's filthy. But, being the little rebel that I was, I asked Aleksandra if we could take a detour and visit Steve. She told me that there was absolutely no chance she would take me there and that my mother would kill her if she found out. I said, "Friends don't hide stuff from each other, Aleks. Are you only our house cleaner, or are you also my friend?" She finally agreed, and off we went.

'I couldn't remember the last time I'd actually left Radlett, so going to Borehamwood was an incredible thrill for me. It felt like I was an adventurer exploring the world. I started cheering uncontrollably as we saw the sign *Welcome to Borehamwood*. Aleksandra merely rolled her eyes in disappointment, and I noticed that she appeared to be stressed out. I wanted to be there as long as possible, so I made sure to display my best behaviour, no matter how excited I was about our little road trip. It was pure wanderlust.

'When Aleksandra drove into the village, I was gobsmacked and almost speechless. "This looks like a different country," I told her, provoking a response of laughter. I stuck my head out of the window while Aleksandra slowed down, adhering to the speed limit. I felt free as a bird on that day. I'd always wanted to travel, and now my time had come. However, my gleaming smile quickly turned to shock and awe as I saw something I couldn't believe, just as we made a left turn into one of the side streets. I had to blink my eyes a number of times to make sure they weren't deceiving me. I screamed, "Stop the car," giving Aleksandra the shock of her life. She then proceeded to slam on the breaks, until the car came to a screeching halt in the middle of the road. I'm not one to mess around, unlike the girl who cried wolf, so Aleksandra knew it wasn't a false alarm. This was the real deal. She looked up and shrieked. We were in the "bad" part of the village. The "filthy" my mother had spoken of. Rubbish was strewn all over the sidewalks and dirty children were roaming the streets like wild animals. Everything made out of metal appeared to be rusted and everything made out of wood appeared to be rotten and faded by the sun. There was a sour stench hanging in the air.

Look, I don't usually act out. I'm always good as gold no matter what the circumstances. So I told myself that I deserved just that one opportunity to act out of character.

'As soon as the car was stationary, I threw a tantrum and then said, "If you don't give me permission to leave the car, I'll open up the door and run, Aleks. I will take matters into my own hands. Her car wasn't modern enough to have child locks. This meant that I could pull the handle and unlock the door myself. She knew she was responsible for me and I was a walking lawsuit. She also understood that I knew I had such powers. Now, the reason for my outburst was that I had a feeling in my stomach that I needed to explore those streets and those houses. Bear in mind, if anything happened to me, Aleksandra's life would be over. My mother would most certainly arrange for her to be deported back to Poland and I knew she didn't want that. She always told me, "It's a better life here in England." This is something I could never understand because I have seen pictures of Poland and it looked beautiful.

'So, in the end, Aleksandra tentatively climbed out of the car with me. She held my hand extra tight as we slowly approached the nearest house. She rang the doorbell reluctantly before saying, "One minute here, and that's it." I agreed to her deal. She was definitely more sceptical than I was about the "bad part of town". The contrast to Radlett was almost unimaginable. No more than a fifteen-minute drive away was our estate, full of mansions. But this street was so different, a place where a girl like me didn't belong. Anyone who lived in houses like these weren't our type of people, but I didn't even know this world existed until Aleksandra took that wrong turn earlier. I'd never seen houses comparable to these ones before. They were so tiny, like doll houses. I guessed then that each house contained only two or three rooms, and I would find out later that I my guess was right. Imagine living in a place with only two floors and having to climb stairs when going to the upper floor instead of using an elevator.

'Looking around, I was still amazed by the fact that the streets were filled with children. *Why did their parents just let them out of the house to play on the sidewalk instead of in the backyard?* I silently asked myself. *Don't they know it's dangerous?*

'A boy my age approached me after kicking a football in my direction. The way he was dressed was so different to what I was used to. He had an air of carelessness about him, and I loved that. There were so many rules in my life and they were clearly not applicable to this scruffy but friendly boy. I was starting to believe that good things happen to those that don't play by the rules. He stopped about twenty yards in front of me and shouted, "Well, aren't you going to kick it back to me, poshy?" I looked down at the football beside me and then asked his name. "Nice to meet you, poshy," he replied confidently. "I'm Peter." I laughed at his funny way of talking. It wasn't the way I'd ever heard anyone speak before. These countryside folks had a much different dialect to the one Mother had taught me. I introduced myself in a shy voice and then asked him, "Where do you live?" He replied, "Newbury Street, born and raised." so I said, "Umm, where is that?" And he replied, "That's the street you're standing on right now, silly." When he asked me the same question, I said "Radlett." "Classic," he responded, "that's where all the poshy's live. Speak some more, I want to hear your poshy accent," he kept urging me on.

'He was fascinated by the way I pronounced my words, so he called his friend sover. "You gotta come hear this, boys!" He continued asking me to repeat sentences such as "The cat sat on the mat" and "Jack and Jill went up the hill." Afterwards they would all laugh with me, never at me. They were so interested in me, it was genuinely the best feeling ever. I didn't really get it at the time, but I was so happy that they were curious about me, so I couldn't care less. They had their bags and coats in the road as markers for the goals in their football game. I asked them why they didn't go to the private soccer practice I attended and they laughed. They said they would have loved to, but they just wanted to have fun. Plus, they said their parents couldn't afford the expensive membership fees.

'They wanted to know if I would like to play with them. I looked at Aleksandra with pleading eyes and she looked back at me. I begged her, "Please, just for a little while." Her heart eventually crumbled and she said, "Go ahead, Victoria. Enjoy and be safe." She cared about my safety a great deal, but she also realised that there were times children merely had to be children.

'So I played soccer in the streets with all these new friends I just made. And they said, "Same time tomorrow?" I shot one glance in Aleksandra's direction and then made the decision for us. I chuckled and told them, "I'll be here."

'I never met Aleksandra's special friend Steve that day; he was out of town for business. But it was the most fun I'd ever had as a child. I had never connected with other kids like that in my life. And that was when I came to the conclusion of just how trapped I was... Because of what? Because of money. Because my mother had so much money that I never got the chance to have an ordinary, joyful childhood. I couldn't experience the Borehamwood way of life. I was locked out of it, because of Betty Allen's goddamn wealth.'

Dr. Williams puts down his notepad and pen. He just stares into my eyes. 'I see, I see,' he says. He looks me up and down. 'Don't you?'

'Don't I what?'

'Don't you see?' he asks again. 'You're Betty. You should be Aleksandra.'

'No, no, no. How? No.' I begin to sob. I can't be in his practice anymore.

I get up and walk out... right back into my living hell.

Chapter 12

The Secret's Out

The years pass without any major incidents and Destiny finally graduates from high school. Instead of going on an extended holiday like the other teenagers, she begins to help out at the Jolly Goat. Destiny gets along better with Strawberry than I am. The men frequenting the pub flirt more with my daughter than with me, because I never got that boob job I wanted. Ever since I opened up to Dr. Williams I've been miserable. His words continue to swim around in my head: 'Don't you see? You're Betty. You should be Aleksandra.'

Billy left a few months ago and the hardships got worse. He left without any explanation. Just like my dad, he simply packed up and vanished. At first I thought it was going to be difficult without him around, but now that it's only me and Destiny in the house I'm kind of glad he is gone. I didn't need him in my life to be a happy woman and because he'd left it meant that I had to teach myself to be all I needed, an independent mother looking after her daughter. It's been painful for her to not want to be as close to me, but I'm sure she will come around. Kids go through phases, it's all quite natural. I shouldn't worry about it too much. I am strong, just like I've taught her to be, and I don't need Billy or Dr. Williams or anybody…

I'm fine… I'm happy… I'm fine.

***

At the tender age of twenty-one, Destiny announces her pregnancy to me. I'm taken aback, but then I remember that we are not among the Crown Jewels of people here in Lansbury. Knowing the men living on this estate, it's maybe more of a shock that it didn't happen sooner.

'Do you know who the father is?' I ask her as politely as I can. 'Is it a boyfriend? Come on, you can talk to me, Destiny. I'm your mother.'

Destiny rolls her eyes, but I can see the tears beginning to form there. She's scared. Of course, she's scared… and confused, and disappointed in herself. The ghosts of my past appear without my permission, as they always do. I remember feeling scared, lost, alone. I don't want that for my precious daughter. I did everything I could to save her from such things, didn't I?

She's so quiet. Why won't she let me in? Aren't I her best friend? Sure, she's gone through some rough stages in her life, but I've always been there for her, so she should trust me. She should trust me in the same way I would have trusted the mother I wished for instead of the one that was bestowed upon me. I've taught Destiny how to be a good, responsible adult.

Now she was going to have a child of her own and I've made peace with it.

I have been hurt and humiliated throughout my life, but my grandchild will give me the inspiration and the strength to keep going. Yes... I am a strong and independent woman, no matter what. I know that I can do it all by myself.

But Destiny not wanting me in her life, not anymore, hurts me in a way I have never experienced before. She is still living under my roof and she won't even speak to me. Billy was her sworn enemy and now so am I, it seems. Destiny is taking all measures possible to keep her distance from me. She is never home during the days, which is odd. Because when I go look for her at the pub, she's also not working. She must be doing something else with someone else.

I decide to dig. It's for her own good and I'm only trying to protect her. Mother knows best after all. She will thank me one day, even though she is being so ungrateful at the moment. She just doesn't realise how far I've gone to keep her safe and happy. If she's decided to be distant for a while, then that's her decision. But if she's in trouble... well, Mother is here for her. Just like when I went through her diary. Imagine what kind of stuff she could have been mixed up in, had I not intervened! And I never would have known about any of her troubles. No, a mother has to do what's necessary, even if not everyone else agrees. Other people don't know Destiny the way I do. They also don't have the experience I have acquired over the years as her mother. I would do anything to give my daughter a better life... *anything*.

I decide to get someone involved who is still on speaking terms with Destiny. If there is anybody to ask, someone who knows everyone's business, it's Strawberry. I need to update her about the Billy situation (or *non*-situation) anyway.

I make my way over to the Jolly Goat to speak to her — in her capacity as a friend, of course, not my boss. The daytime Civilian Strawberry is much easier to talk to than the night-time While-I'm-on-shift Strawberry.

'What are you doing here, Brenda?' Strawberry says with a fake smile. 'Your shift only starts at five, my dear.' She's standing behind the cash register, busy counting money.

I put my handbag down on the bar counter and sigh. 'I have some news for you.'

'News?' she says, frowning. 'I hope it's good.'

Without hesitation, I just spit it out: 'Billy broke up with me.'

Strawberry approaches me and touches my arm. She seems sincerely sorry for me, even though I don't have any emotion on my face. I don't even have any feelings about it anymore.

'You know I'm here for you no matter what,' Strawberry says, 'and whenever you're ready to talk, I'm here to listen.' This gesture is very sweet. It's the first time she's hearing about the breakup and she obviously thinks that I am distraught.

'I'm totally over it,' I tell her. 'Honestly, I am. Don't worry about me, I'm going to be just fine. It's been a couple of months already and I haven't thought about him or missed him at all. In fact, I was glad to see the back of him. It was strange how it all happened.'

'Oh, this occurred months ago?' Strawberry says, furrowing her brow. There is a lengthy pause before she resumes. 'How come I see him every day on the estate with Destiny then?'

'You fucking what?' I shout, feeling my blood beginning to boil.

I storm out of the pub in a rage.

How could I not have known about this? Destiny still doesn't know I checked her diary. She writes in it nearly every day. That's all she does in her room all evening instead of doing what is right and having meaningful conversations with her mother. I have to take things into my own hands once again, because all those years ago I did it for a good reason and this right here is another good one. I have to find out what is going on and it will be better this time, since Billy isn't around to judge me for my actions. What could he be up to? Turning her against me, perhaps. With men you can never be sure what to expect.

Yes, this is my only option. I don't know what else to do. I simply can't trust Destiny anymore. I can't stand any more of her lies and her blatant deception. This is the only way I can be sure of the truth...

***

While she is out gallivanting the next day I take it upon myself to enter her room, quietly like the previous time. She still has her stupid DO NOT DISTURB sign hanging on the doorknob. I ignore it, ease the door open and step inside. I rummage through her cupboards until I eventually locate her diary. I find it funny how she thinks if she stores it in a different place nobody would discover it. She's never been very good at hiding things.

The diary looks different, though. It has a new cover and the message on the front has changed. It now reads: *Brenda Miracle please read carefully.*

My palms start to sweat and my anxiety begins to kick in. My eyes are blurry. It's like I have tunnel vision. Everything around me blackens. What the hell is going on?

I take a deep breath and fight off the evil demons in my mind. I need to have a clear head. I need to try to understand this. Destiny obviously knows I looked through her diary. But how?

Billy.

Shit.

He must have told her about what I did all those years ago, which means she also knows that I'm the one who destroyed her dolls. No wonder she hates me so much.

I open the next page, expecting the unexpected.

I start to read

Brenda,

You are not my mother anymore.

You are a terrible person and I swear to never speak to you ever again in my life. You invaded my privacy while I was growing up, and that's something I'll never forgive you for. You destroyed my dolls while you knew they were my best friends. And you just watched me cry. What kind of an evil beast are you? You disgust me. Yes, Billy told me about that sick secret. And the night I saw you getting slapped, I felt for you. I actually suffered with you. It hurt me. I can never condone physical violence, in any situation, but now I understand that you deserved to be put in your place, because I know your secret.

After Billy told me that you were withholding something from our family, I did a bit of investigating. And you're not the only one who can snoop around other people's business. I can do it, too. So here you go. I was looking through your drawers. You must have completely forgotten that you even had it, but I found an envelope. It was titled: 'Last will and testament of Betty Allen'. I'm assuming this was the grandmother I wasn't allowed to know ever existed. The text was in a legally binding format and it said: 'I hereby revoke any previous wills and codicils. I devise, bequeath and give all that I own, including my family estate, to my biological granddaughter.

You evil cow. You crossed out the part that says grand, so that you would get all the money. I'm not stupid. You're a heartless bitch. I just can't connect these dots. How you would be so cruel and let me suffer my entire life. So here's my final message to you.

Yes, I'm pregnant, and you'll never get to meet your grandchild.

Oh, and something else... Billy. Well, Billy is the father.

Revenge is sweet.

Have a nice life, you psychotic beast.

Oh shit... I'm fucked.

Chapter 13

An Early Marriage

High School was rough when I was growing up. Everyone was so snobby. I wasn't like them, and I refused to pretend that I was. I would not be a part of their conformity.

Now, some things should be said here. If you are a wallflower, you are not alone. You're one of many in society. Those who take this status well will become observers. Ironically, society thinks it confines us within its norms. But no. We are stronger when we bear witness.

The walls were built by wallflowers for wallflowers, from philosophies to capricious fads. We measure the extent of society's influence and then position ourselves far from its reach. We could choose to overrun society, but we take our time. We have our own ideas and outlook. We could choose to abandon society to its own devices or we could form ourselves into a pretty bouquet of individual flowers, whichever most benefit us.

If we allow it, society would flock to us like bees and suck us dry of our sweet nectar. That is why we stay where we are. We blend into the walls, lest we abscond on our power to overtake society's growth with our tough, grass-root identities. Individuality seems to be discouraged at school, but pride — pride seems to be key. The definition of pride, though, seems to change on a whim. Sometimes it's wearing the same sweater, and sometimes it's something... I don't know... something else, something more. If any rational person such as myself were to look at the simple, basic, average adult, it was the same. Thinking for oneself takes so much work. And then, who are you able to blame for the consequences? There is power in groupthink; cliques, as I already mentioned. It's just in the hands of those controlling it. I am in control, but I never bear responsibility. I am a filter. To others, a leader. But to myself, I've distilled the wisdom of others into objective truths. However, there is one thing for sure: I never felt like I needed to rely on dolls to keep me company and give me a sense of belonging. I have at times, though, felt as if I had to play the game. And if that meant sacrificing who I was, then I was totally fine with it.

I told Peter of Borehamwood that I needed to clean him up, so that he would fit in with the 'poshies,' as he used to call us. Not that I would usually care to show my boyfriend off to anyone, but I still wanted to do the cleaning up, for *me*. I wanted to go out on a whim. And my high school prom dance was the best way of doing so. It was about self-respect and having pride in myself.

The week before my prom, my mother had actually ordered me a pastel pink ball gown. Lucky me. I wore silver heels and clutched a dazzling sequined purse. The other girls were so jealous, you could see it in their eyes, I promise you.

My school was upper class and we did everything like the Americans. The prom king was a tight race between Peter or a guy in my year named Larry. Larry was a ladies' man, extremely good-looking. But the girls in my school had never met a guy like Peter before, so they were intrigued by his mannerisms. I also felt like I had a good enough chance to be prom queen going with Peter. It was a popularity contest after all, like everything else in my life was at that stage. Destiny was different as a child, though. While the others were laughing at her and playing the game, she was playing with her precious dolls, her precious friends...her *only* friends.

I knew it was all a game back then. I could control it, and I did. I was no longer alone once I figured this out. My mother was alone. Peter was alone. I've also learned from an early age that being with someone does not necessarily imply that you're not alone. You could be sitting next to someone, holding their hand, and you could both still be desperately alone.

That's not how it turned out for me, not in the end.

At prom, despite him being my date, I blended in with the walls (they were covered in sequins, so my bag did as well) and Peter with the crowd. He spent most of the night flirting with other girls while he knew I was there, watching him. I don't think it was on purpose, but he made me feel like I could have control over being invisible. If I wanted to be seen, all I had to do was wrap my arm around his waist, throw my head back, laugh, and let my cheek settle on his shoulder. Then everybody would know he was mine.

Peter kept telling me he didn't know I could dance so well. I felt that was sort of rude. Before the prom, when he showed up at our house with rose-gold cufflinks, to match my dress, my mother and Antione gave Peter a pep talk. I'm not sure what it was about, and I now kind of hope I never find out.

We drove to the prom in Peter's father's old hatchback — another glaring symbol that they were not as well off as Peter would have liked them to be. He drove incredibly slow while glancing at me every thirty seconds. I wouldn't indulge him beyond the way I honestly felt.

We looked so fucking good that night. The golden couple, they called us. But we were far away from each other in the beginning. Anyway, we won prom king and queen. Everyone was congratulating us. It was wonderful, except that many of the congratulations — particularly from some of the boys — contained a hint of 'Right? Right?' Like they assumed we were going to go to the after party, then ride into the sunset and get married. I didn't like the sound of that, even though we were already officially dating by then.

I still remember when he first asked me out.

'Excuse me. Victoria?' he said. He was gentle, polite, and slightly out of breath. It happened on a windy day after a game of football in the streets of Borehamwood.

At that point in my high school career, I felt as if I was finally emerging from a cocoon, and I don't just mean puberty. There was certain a switch in confidence as well. I had chosen to grow up. And it wasn't necessarily a good feeling when I first saw Peter. It was like poisonous butterflies — or large grotesque moths, like those horrid ones in Australia — flying around in my stomach. I think some people also thought that I was a poisonous butterfly.

But if poisonous butterflies know they are poisonous butterflies, they can act like poisonous butterflies, and in that display of power is control. Some days, I feel like I can rule the world. Others, I feel like the awkward, shy little girl that I have always been in front of my mother. His ignorance of me never really helped in that department.

Anyway, where was I... Peter... Ah yes, Peter, that sweet boy. He asked me to be his date in front of all those boys and girls without even blushing. I never would have dreamed that someone like Peter would ask me out, but he did. In fact, he said he had been meaning to ask me for weeks before he finally found the bravado to do it. After our third date, a movie in the park, he kissed me for the first time, then said, 'Hey, poshy' and told me he was in love with me.

In retrospect, I'm impressed that I didn't just think he was after my school notes. He was after me, after my body and my soul. Peter was the sidekick of this punk chap named David Lewis. David was better looking than Peter but a bit of an ass. He never asked me out. His father was a plumber and, as you can imagine, it trickles down, so he didn't have much as far as being wealthy was concerned. Peter was spoiled compared to him. Peter acted spoiled. It was his way of 'fitting in'. He was always a day behind in matching what Larry wore to school. If David wore a polo-neck jersey on Monday, Peter wore a polo-neck jersey on Tuesday, while David was wearing a V-neck sweater. Then Peter wore a V-neck sweater on Wednesday, while David was wearing an ironed button-down shirt, and so on and so on.

I doubt if Peter remembered later in life how desperate he came off on that windy day. But to me it was rather charming. We were such silly kids back then. Once he had asked me out, I told Peter that I would think about it. He persisted by saying he wanted an answer right away. He promised and promised me that he would not get mad if I said no. He swore that he would respect my honest feelings. I held him off for another 24 hours. By then his mystery had worn off just a bit and I had to see if I could figure out a way to keep my interest. Of course, I ended up finding some and — while I doubt he expected it — he did as well. I made him sweat and he made me guess where he was taking me for our first date.

He treated me like a princess, you know, just the way a girl is supposed to be treated. Although I don't really have anything else to compare it to. In all honesty, I like the idea of being a real-life princess one day. Imagine how expansive my tiara collection would be. And I don't mean it in the fairy-tale sense that a child might dream of. No, I mean royalty. The real kind of royalty. So much for my theory of minimalism, right?

Although we looked like a golden couple on prom night, we were as far away from each other as two stars in a constellation. Everybody was wishing us well, as if we would be together for the rest of our lives. Little did I know then that I would end up marrying Peter simply because he made me look good in front of other people and I loved it.

'I want to have children with you, Victoria. I want you to be their mother.' That was how he proposed. Not "Will you marry me?" or "Please be my bride?" Children.

I could forgive Peter for wanting me to submit at that time. It was his way to reinforce his masculinity against the possibility of rejection. He would insist on getting his way. It was not up to me, it was up to Peter, or that was how we quietly understood the balance of the power between us. I pretended to be led by Peter, because Peter didn't know any other way but to lead. The problem wasn't that he could not follow, because he could. It was that Peter couldn't follow a person; he needed to follow an ideal, a philosophy. He was forever stuck in a room filled with his imaginative ideas and that was problematic. I've never told him this. No one has.

Peter's father arranged the wedding and we got married in September.

There was only a formal wedding ceremony, no reception or party afterwards. The priest gave us his blessings and then we drove off. The sun was about to set when we reached our destination — an antiquated but still grand hotel. Peter kept holding my hand and he was especially careful with his movements, always allowing me to go through doors first. I was now his wife and he made sure I was aware of this new status.

After we had dinner, we went out onto the hotel's balcony where a jazz band was playing. We listened to three or four songs but I wanted to stay longer, so Peter decided to go to the bar to have a drink. After an hour of blissful music in my ears, I left the balcony and went to the bar to join my husband. Peter was already on his third drink when I arrived. There was someone with him, a man with curly dark hair and elf-like ears. When he turned to face me, I recognized him immediately. It was Peter's friend, David, the douchebag.

***

Peter told me that there was no need for me to work for a living after college, but I had other plans. So his father enrolled me in a personality development course to punish me. The course was for women who had strong opinions and free spirits. I was never one of these women, so I would go on to fail dismally. I objected because I was tricked into attending the course. Peter's father thanked my mother and complimented me for my 'strange wit' but 'wit, just the same.' I knew all along what he was trying to insinuate. He meant that I didn't need to think for myself. He wanted me to be docile and to support Peter's political career.

I must've had the 'right' personality in his dad's mind. The woman who had no opinions, no willpower, and no money to support her dreams was the woman with the 'right' personality for his son. I hated Peter's father, but the problem was that I had started to love Peter. We had many lovely conversations during our short marriage. He would always take the time to seriously consider (by seriously consider, I mean we engaged in full-on debates) my point of view on political and global issues. It was unexpected in the beginning. I was bewildered by the mere notion of Peter consulting me on such important matters. However, he always kept silent about his father's uncalled-for interventions. That was a mystery I could not solve.

Peter knew exactly how to fulfil a woman's wants and needs. One starry night in particular sticks out to me. I wore lace lingerie. I often did, and I would feel remiss if I didn't note that down for posterity's sake. The lights were dimmed and a cosy fire was crackling in the fireplace in our lounge. The whole atmosphere was sexy. He was tender. There was a kindness in his eyes. I can imagine it as I'm sitting here. It was so utterly like that of a doll's long-lash eyes, except his were soft and poppable. Not that I wanted to harm him, it's just a thought I had now. Perhaps because a doll's eyes are so hard and plastic and sewn on, nothing at all like human eyes. Having just written that last sentence feels rather ridiculous to have even put down in writing. But here it shall stay.

I think Peter was following his idea of love making and he was doing his best to share it with me. He was leading me to it and I liked it. I took off Peter's shirt. He did not hesitate at my touch. He buried his face in my neck, and we began.

***

I was invited to the house where Peter had grown up for dinner one evening. I think it was about two years after we'd gotten married. I was ecstatic. I didn't ever have sit-down meals with my mother, so I always relished the opportunity to make Peter's family mine, regardless of the fact that I didn't like his dad. It felt like the right thing to do. Sometimes I would think about how my father didn't come to my wedding. I would think about this in the kind of generalized way where you compare yourself to the 'norm.' But then I would comfort myself and remember that my father never really did his job, so why should he have deserved to see me wed anyway?

They were all acting a little off during that dinner; Peter as well as his mother and father. I couldn't quite put my finger on it.

Then, after the main course, Peter's mum told me, 'Victoria, as much as we enjoy your company and love having you around for dinner, there is some news we need to break to you.'

Peter added, 'And you're probably not going to like it.'

I prepared myself for the absolute worst case scenario. Don't get me wrong, I wasn't expecting Peter to file a divorce. *But if that is what I'm about to hear,* I silently thought, *not like this, please. Not in front of your parents, Peter. How brutal can you be?*

Then all three of them started talking at the same time. They were stumbling on their words and treading on eggshells. They needed to find the right way to explain the bad news to me and I've hated those types of situations my whole life. They have always caused me immense anxiety. I told them to skip the build-up and lay it on me. I can't bear it when people are building up to a climax, especially not a climax of bad news. It adds unnecessary anticipation as well as pressure. So, Peter's mother finally told me that her husband had been doing some research and that he thought my father's disappearance was a tad suspicious. Then Peter said that they suspected my mother of killing my father.

'Come again?' I'd asked, knocking over a glass of wine.

They soon launched into a conspiracy theory which consisted of what I considered to be very loose points. I listened respectfully but also had to fight to keep the shock from showing on my face. I didn't want to disappoint Peter's family by giving them the impression of me thinking that they were lying. What shocked me the most was the casual way they spoke about it, as if they were simply airing out their ideas. I nodded in all the right places during their explanations, restraining the urge to wander off into another daydream filled with the small collection of memories of my father I still carried around in my head. When they were finished, they simply moved on to dessert, as naturally as on any other night around the dinner table.

I still hadn't heard anything from my father for years at that stage. My mother said it was because he didn't love us anymore. She had definitely moved on. She was happy with Antione. She spoiled him like the son she never had. Mother introduced Antione to her friends on the phone as 'the prince she wants to marry one day.' She always tried to avoid calling him this in front of me, but I've heard her say it when she thought I wasn't listening. He brought my mother a bouquet of white lilies once. I don't think he or she realised how much that had hurt me. Lilies used to be my dad's favourite flowers.

The closest I ever came to making contact with him again was when I found his journal. It was hidden behind a stack of tin rusk containers in one of the kitchen cupboards, together with a letter carrying a 'return to sender' message on a flaky envelope. The stamps on the letter displayed pictures of pink flamingos on the shore of some lake. I had never heard him talk about flamingos before, but I'd like to think he would have adored them.

I was afraid to open the letter and remained that way, even though there was a possibility that reading it could break the illusion I had constructed of my mother. But it didn't feel like an illusion. It felt real. Either it had always been or I had believed it for so long that it was indecipherable. Perhaps I was deserving of the way I felt. Perhaps I did drive my father away. He'd once mistaken me as a damn demon, after all. But, then again, maybe I was a demon then and still am one today. While reading my dad's journal (nothing too revealing in there) it made me sad to think about him, but I was used to the pain of sadness. I was completely immune at that point. I didn't want to shatter any of the truths, or illusions for that matter.

So I took the letter but never opened it.

***

Peter always had a dream of going to university to further his studies. Despite his financial struggles, he was determined to overcome any barriers he might face in realising this dream. By then I was working at a day-care centre, against his father's will, and I offered to help Peter pay for his tuition fees. He graciously accepted, but that's when things began to go very wrong. It all went to hell after I started giving him money.

He felt too dependent on me and he couldn't handle the fact that *my* money paid for more than seventy percent of his university fees. Over the next six months, things came to a close with Peter. One day he just ran away. As men do.

I think it was a combination of the money and a feeling of suffocation.

When I started having my night terrors, he was freaked out. I kept grabbing him in my sleep, mistaking him for the demons from my dreams. After we'd gotten married, I became overbearing to Peter, I'll admit. He kept complaining that I would suffocate him and that he didn't have any time to live his life anymore. My love for him was all-encompassing and became like a drug to me. And I took it too far. But anyway, the one day he was there and the next day he was gone. Just like that. It took me only a short while to tell myself, "Good riddance." If he couldn't love me for who I was and work through the problems with me, then I didn't need him. No woman ever needs a man, that's what I believe today.

***

Revenge.

I don't think I'm a very revengeful individual, but I do like to get even. And after Peter walked out on me like that, it was time to get even. I went to a music festival a week later and there I found a rather dashingly handsome boy, the lead guitarist of some band whose name I was unable to pronounce. We became tipsy and decided to get into each other's pants. I thought there was going to be romance and candles, waves crashing on beaches and trains going through tunnels. You know, the whole works, just like the bits in the movies that you don't get to see. But it was nothing like that. It happened in a dilapidated, unused ticket sales office building behind the main stage.

And that's how I became pregnant.

Nine months later, Destiny came into my life.

But she was right — she wasn't a miracle.

Chapter 14

My Mothercare Reality

I come home from the Jolly Goat one day to find my car gone, along with my dearest essentials. I will have to phone Destiny and let her know that this will be the very last time she ever steals my beer and my cigarettes. Even though she may be reluctant, Destiny knows to always answer my calls. I raised her that way and I trust that she will remember that.

I call, but she doesn't answer, which pisses me off at first. The feeling gradually goes away and now I'm worried about her. Why wouldn't she answer her cell phone? I call again. She still doesn't answer. Something is up, but I can't figure it out from where I'm standing in my living room. Some say I tend to over-dramatize things, but in reality I have reason to be worried. I decide to act fast.

Going to the little printing shop down the road, I pay them to print fifty flyers with a recent photograph of Destiny's face and the words MISSING WOMAN, followed by my telephone number. I stick the flyers all over Tower Hamlets and call the police to arrange a search party to look for her. The police insist on starting with an extensive search at my property. I bluntly refuse. One of the uniformed officers asks me if I have anything sensitive in the house that he should know of. I politely ask them to leave. Their search is over.

Once the officers are gone, I check my bedside drawer, thinking about the 'anything sensitive' the police officer mentioned. I open the drawer and peek inside. My mother's testament is missing. Destiny must have taken it with her after she wrote me that ugly letter.

My phone rings on the dining room table downstairs, where I've left it earlier.

I run down to answer the call in time. It might be my daughter calling me back.

When I look at the screen, I see that my hunch was right. The call is from Destiny.

'Where the hell are you?' I shout as a way of answering.

'You know where I am,' she replies.

'Radlett?'

'Yes, Brenda Bitch, Radlett. I'm hunting for the treasure with Billy. I've hired a lawyer and I am going to have him prove that the will was tampered with while your mother was on her deathbed. I will search every single house in Radlett if I have to. You won't get away with this.'

I don't respond to anything she has said. She must have grown impatient because ten seconds later she hangs up. I'm left wondering what to do next. *Burn it…* a voice in the back of my mind whispers, then begins to grow louder. *You must burn it all!* Is this what mania feels like? I've read about such things. There was a time when I thought I could do some research and figure out exactly what had gone wrong with my father. I didn't get very far, though, and my mother was certainly of no help.

I will destroy everything and then Destiny will learn she can't treat her own mother this way. How could she be so ungrateful… after all that I've done for her. And Billy… where the hell does he get the nerve? I thought I knew him, but he's just like all the others. All the men in my life have turned out to be cut from the same disgusting cloth. None of them ever took responsibility, they just ran from their problems the moment things got tough.

My hands begin to tremble as I feverishly search online for how to create a sizable blast… to make it look like an accident. Perhaps propane, a malfunction with the stove. It says here… yes, I can let the place fill with gas then set a trigger to ignite it. The banknotes will quickly burn to ashes. *This will be a lesson you won't soon forget, my dear daughter.*

***

Over the course of the next two days, I purchase what I need using a few separate accounts and delivery addresses near my old home in Radlett. I'm extremely careful and move only at night, back and forth between the hotel I'm staying at and my house where the money remains undisturbed in the attic. The memories and ghosts threaten to overtake me once more, but I am able to push everything aside in favor of what must be done. I must focus… it will all be over soon.

On the third night, I am finally ready to bury the house and its curse. On my way there I become a little worried as the first raindrops of a shower begin to fall. However, it doesn't look like it will get too heavy. Nothing can stop me now. A bit of rain won't get in the way of the furnace I'm going to create in that house. It could even help destroy some of the evidence that might be left behind, although I've been careful not to cut corners. This is one of the most important tasks I will ever complete, after all. One day, my daughter and grandchild will see me as their savior. Destiny may not know and appreciate what I'm doing for her tonight, but in the months to come, she will surely realise that I've saved her from a terrible mess.

The poison of money seeps into one's veins and one can never escape it. I won't see my daughter turn into the slimy, money-riddled monster my mother became. She deserves so much more, and she will have it.

Because I have kept an eye on the neighborhood, I've noticed the pattern Destiny and Billy have been following to go from house to house. They have been zeroing in on the right location, so I know I have to pull this off tonight.

Once I'm inside my old house I work fast and efficiently, first securing all the places where gas might leak out with duct tape, and then opening the nozzles of the six medium-sized gas cylinders I've bought. Within an hour, everything is in place. Now I just have to wait a while to allow the interior to fill up with gas. The stuff is oozing into my nose and burning my lungs.

I swiftly set the trigger (equipped with an electronic timer) to ignite the propane, then hurry through the front door until I'm safely outside. It's almost over now… almost.

As I stand in the driveway outside my old home, the ghosts make their way into my mind once again, begging me to stop doing what I'm doing. The voices tell me I don't know what I'm doing, but I know exactly what I'm doing. No one is going to tell me I haven't done it right this time. I'm the only one strong enough to do what needs to be done.

'Brenda!' a voice sounds from somewhere nearby… and it's not one of the ghosts.

No, wait, I know this voice.

'Brenda!'

I turn to see Billy running toward me from across the street.

'Brenda, what are you doing?" he asks in a panic, once he reaches me. 'You have to go get Destiny! She's inside! I smelled the gas but she's determined to get all the evidence. Whatever you're planning, you have to stop it!' The alarm in his voice strikes fear into my heart.

I hear the words but I have trouble processing the reality of what he has just said.

You still have time, my subconscious tells me.

'My baby!' I scream, but my nerves are so shot I can barely hear my own voice. 'Destiny! I'm coming, baby! You have to get out of there!' I command my jelly legs to move and I'm ready to break into a sprint when the world comes to an end.

The blast lights up the sky with a terrifying brilliance while a booming sound rocks the entire neighborhood.

At first I'm certain I've gone deaf, but then I hear it — a sound that will haunt me for the rest of my days: a child's cry. But no, she is a young woman now, and that voice… that horrific scream… filled with the intensity of agony I have never heard before.

The sickening thought starts from far away and then grows closer, until the whisper of madness speaks clearly in my ears… or perhaps it is my mother, my father and all the other voices I've shoved away for so many years. *What have you done, Brenda?*

Billy is yelling. I regret that my sense of hearing is returning and now I listen to the desperate cries of a man I was once in love with. The man of my dreams, with the tattoos and the smart way of speaking to Destiny as a child… now her lover, an expecting father… now a devastated and broken human being.

I melt down beside him while the gentle rain tries to kill the flames in vain. I can hear sirens coming from the other side of town, but I know it is too late.

She was inside, the voices berate me over and over, *she was inside the bloody house, you fucking monster…*

Beyond the voices, memories of my beautiful baby girl arrive to torture me even further. They are determined to find a punishment fitting for such a heinous act. I hear the first coos of my only child, her first laugh and her first words. I see myself dressing her up for her first day at school. I see the line of dolls she has set up for her tea parties. Her smiling up at me from a time long gone. She was once an innocent child who trusted her mother with all her heart. The life I've built so carefully for her has disappeared in the flames of hell that *I* have created.

What happens next is a reminder of what I have become.

At first I think there are angels beginning to swirl around me, then I realise they are burning banknotes floating from the sky; the last remains of a fortune I have kept hidden for years. The dying breath of that fortune is now pitifully falling down as embers in the light rain.

It has already taken its toll and now it will leave me to linger in sorrow forever.

Chapter 15

I Have Become My Mother

It is a new world and God has decided to let me live in it.

I suppose it's what I deserve. I have not functioned properly since that night and I know that in order to keep bearing this punishment, I need help to keep on going forward. I dial a familiar phone number and make an appointment with Dr. Rupert Williams.

'Brenda, I was surprised to hear from you,' he says once I'm seated in his consultation room. 'Tell me, what's going on? You look, uhm, different. Have you been eating and sleeping all right? Why are you so pale?' His concern may have been endearing to one with hope.

'I've killed her, Dr. Williams. I've killed my only daughter and her unborn child. They have left this world in the most terrifying way possible… and it is all my fault. Please tell me something: how am I supposed to keep on living?'

Dr. Williams sits dumbfounded for what seems like an eternity before starting to connect the dots in his mind. The story was all over the news, after all. The fire here in Radlett… at an address that is recorded on my patient file. Piles of money burned and one — no, two —casualties.

'Brenda, I'm…'

I understand. There is really nothing to say. No one can help me anymore.

A couple of minutes go by and there is absolute silence between us. Eventually, my mind starts to form coherent thoughts and I begin a reprise of all those dreams and memories that once seemed so mysterious.

Dr. Williams drops his voice to barely above a whisper and says, 'Do you see, perhaps, some similarities? I mean, think about your relationship with your daughter. It's hard, but there are parallels to be drawn between you and your…' His words trail off.

And I see it. It's crystal clear. It's like being hit by a freight train. I see what has been happening to me my entire adult life. Since giving birth to Destiny I've tried so incredibly hard to escape the chains binding me to my mother, yet they've been there the whole time. I was merely fooling myself to think I would free myself from her. What a catastrophe! Yes, I see it now. And I deserve to feel this way. I deserve to feel empty inside.

'I understand what you're saying, Dr. Williams.' My voice sounds stifled. 'How can I…'

That's as far as I can get, then the tears begin to stream down my face. They won't stop and soon I am sobbing. I reach for my phone. It's time to do the right thing. I'm going to dial the number for the police. I am a murderer… like my…

But, just as so many times before in this office, I become overwhelmed. I stand up from the chair and, without a goodbye, explanation, or apology storm out the door. I am running so fast, I feel as if I might fall and break something. But I keep on running… running. Whatever it is I'm running from, the knowledge of being a killer laughs at me from behind. I know I can never get away. I may as well be running in circles.

Many of us define our successes by our achievements. Our inflated egos keep us afloat. How we feel about ourselves, the difference we make in other people's lives, and a sense of belonging is what brings us happiness. Imagine the sudden realisation — and the pain it causes — that all your efforts to raise and protect your daughter have gone to waste.

I am what I set out to avoid being my entire life.

Being the best mum was all I ever wanted.

But I became the monster.

Chapter 16

In the News

A woman once known in the former as Victoria Allen and in the latter as Brenda Miracle has perished by the whim of her own hand. Her body was discovered in Hilfield Park reservoir lake, Radlett, yesterday afternoon. Early indications show that she had drowned herself.

In what police now call a bizarre murder-suicide case, Victoria's daughter, Destiny, was also found dead at a house nearby, only four days ago. The pathologist's autopsy report specifies that she was ten weeks pregnant at the time.

A close friend of the family, Mr. Billy Bateman, told the police that Victoria set fire to the house while her daughter was inside. This was done intentionally, he further said, because of a supposed money-related conflict between Destiny and her mother.

The metropolitan police have confirmed there is reason to believe that hundreds of millions of Pounds in cash had been inside the house as it burned to the ground.

While no one else suffered any major physical injuries, firemen rushed to the scene to extinguish the flames in the posh neighborhood. One of the neighbours had called the emergency services upon hearing an explosion and seeing the house on fire. Investigators continue to work to nail down the details of the blast and subsequent fire, although the head of police said in a statement to the press that the only suspect at the moment is Victoria Allen.

Chapter 17

A Suicide Note

To all the mourners and everyone else reading:

Learn from my mistakes.

This is my mothercare nightmare that I will now never wake up from.

To my daughter, Destiny, you were an angel. Your life was snatched away too early because of me. Yes, I know it's too late, but I am deeply sorry for all the pain that I have caused you. I broke the most important promise a mother can make to her child. I said I would never hurt you, no matter what. I've always tried so hard, but I just couldn't seem to get it right.

The world is a beautiful, euphoric place for some. For others, however, our nightmares begin the moment we open our eyes. Some of us suffer because our families make our lives cruel and unforgiving, whilst others are loved and nurtured and see the world as bright beauty.

We often have a huge impact on the people we know. Every action we take, no matter how big or small, may affect our friends and our families. Ultimately, everything we do counts. In all our decisions, from our spoken words to our actions, we make choices: Do we want to be a part of the world's problems or its solutions? I know which one I was part of...

How ironic. My entire life was spent dedicated to chasing the pursuit of happiness and look at where I ended up. Over the years I became so distracted in my attempt to learn from the mistakes of my childhood that I never had the time to discover who I really was. I formed an image of what constituted happiness in my head and, when I finally experienced it, I discovered that it wasn't what I wanted at all.

The world can be so chaotic and it can drag you into dark corners. Life takes you on a rollercoaster you have to ride until it comes to a standstill, or until you decide to jump off. The problem I faced jumping off was losing touch with myself in the process. It wasn't the money all along, it was me, myself and I. Revenge guided me to my final destination.

Wealth has no say over whether we live a happy or empty life. This is determined by our relationships with other people, those giving us meaning and purpose above everything else.

You may ask, 'What if it's all meaningless?'

The answer is easy: it simply isn't. Nothing is ever meaningless. That's why you have to make the most out of your time here on earth. Life is never about faith or gut feel guiding your morals, it is about being a good person.

The world is a big confusing place. We often have difficulty in explaining poverty and suffering. But, no matter where you're from, or how much money you have, you always have the human right to be happy. However, that must come from within you. And I've learned the hard way that it only happens when you are yourself and follow your dreams.

-Victoria

www.ingramcontent.com/pod-product-compliance
Lightning Source LLC
Chambersburg PA
CBHW071626080526
44588CB00010B/1282